So Long...

and thanks for all the material!

By Kilha McQueen

GW00390841

For [b]

Content

On Love, Lust and Co-dependency

On Nature

On Mental Health

On Holidays and Milestones

Final Words...

If You Can Imagine It, You Can Achieve It - 227

Forward

I have been excitedly anticipating this debut collection from Kilha for many years and now it is finally here, it does not disappoint.

At its core, it is an autobiography walking us through the highs and lows of an eventful life, but it is so much more too. It is Kilha's reflections on those life experiences that take us on a journey that keeps us gripped.

Although the book talks us through the people who have come and gone in her life, it is her personal narrative that is the inspirational force throughout.

She is honest, sometimes brutal, always vulnerable, but also clear and inquisitive, dividing each section up and placing them under the magnifying glass to examine like a space traveller or visiting alien, observing from a distance, allowing for her and our growth.

A clever fit for the title's reference to the Hitchhiker's Guide too.

For the longest time, struggling with dyslexia, ADHD, and PTSD, Kilha did not believe that she had the credentials to call herself a poet, let alone that she could be a published poet. But it is in those battles that we see her blossom and watch her writing go from strength to strength, point blank refusing to allow labels to define her, her work or place limitations on who she could or has become.

Kilha's biggest challenge was not writing the book, it was sharing what she had written with the world. Adversity overcome the book's purpose of existence, like her, is to simply acknowledge the truth, and from that, this poignant poetry is born. They are synonymous with each other; one cannot exist without the other.

I first met Kilha, many years ago when we would perform spoken word at open mic events together. I still remember her anxiety and nervousness taking to the stage.

But true to her written word, she never gave in to the fear, and I have watched her become a force to be reckoned with both off and on the mic. Despite that fear of public speaking, her enthusiasm for writing and performing poetry has kept her going. Her compelling way of communicating raw emotion and painful narratives is what has kept the audience engaged and what will keep you, the reader, too.

Although written retrospectively, the voice is live and present, which we bear witness to, enabling the reader's own healing.

This collection is a private but sophisticated creation, made up of everything the experience of being a poet, an artist and a woman fighting back against the demon's life has thrown at her offers.

The values, cultural references and themes all speak for themselves whilst constructing a story that has needed to be told.

It is more than a communication of words but rather a construction of different worlds that all exist to represent both the history of individuals and their unique effects on others.
The healing is in the sharing.

'So Long' takes us through how love in its various forms seems to have become endangered. The book revolves around the many people that Kilha has encountered on her life's journey, and we are reminded that our history is made up of the people around us.

Kilha delights in keeping us humble and tangibly close to all the things that we often lose sight of.

We are educated and given insights on real life situations, yet never deviating from the musicality of the poems. The conversation speaks to you in succinct but intriguing ways about meaningful and memorable moments that become the stories we recite. The poetry is passionate and allows us to reflect on our own authentic but imperfect selves.

Her vulnerabilities display an authenticity you cannot help but ponder and by sharing her story, we are set an example of how empowering it can be to observe and grow.

It is not about bringing up old memories, but about reframing the experiences to see what you have gained rather than lost. And in that, this book is not about a woman who fought; rather it is a brilliant example of a woman who thrived when she changed her mindset, setting a vital example of how we can all soar when we learn to believe in ourselves.

Charnjit Gill

@cgillpoetry

Writing a thank you to the people who made this book possible would probably take me as long as writing this book did and could never do justice to what they have meant to me.

Poetry has been a journey that I have been blessed to travel only with the kind support of those around me. If I were to name a few of those souls they would include Carla, Becca, Tim, Mohini, Charni, Tannika, Suzy, Rocco, the girls, the idiot, Asia, Flora, you, all the women who have led by example, all the supportive souls within the poetry community and the many, many angels I have been lucky enough to encounter on my journey who have demonstrated the power in kindness rather than criticizing.

I dedicate this body of work to those no longer here, to all my dyslexic, ADHD and PTSD brothers and sisters who start the race from exhausted each day but still get up and run it; and to anyone who saw beneath the banshee...

Thank you!

This was only ever possible because of you.

Love Kilha x

Typos are the scars of a dyslexic poet

Kilha

Intro

Raison d'etre

Poetry is a reflection of a life lived
Magnified through an individual
Single
Teardrop
Falling from joy
Or
From pain

Its personal accountability mirrored back
Through self-awareness
Forgiving ourselves
For our humanity
Without the attached addiction to shame

It's the vision to see
Inside the accepted
Capturing the extraordinary
With nothing but these ordinary words
and to release them
like a beacon
Calling home anyone who resonates with the
messages that they have heard

It is not a way to be cool
It is not an excuse to be mean
It is not a way to pick up chicks
Or form cliques
Or justify misguided deeds
 It is not an easy option
It is not a get rich quick scheme
It is not a right
And it shouldn't be a fight
It's the communion of a community
Who share in a love of verbal alchemy

It is tragedy turned into beauty
It is compassion for battles others have still to
overcome
It's an education for hearts still open to learning
It is the unification of a polarised world
To come together and start existing as one

To be a poet is both a blessing and a curse
Feeling everything
And everything
With a raging force
Like a fire
That burns against naked skin
It's an obsession
It's our expression
It's the be all and end all of everything we think

To be a poet has been my life's calling
My raison d'etre is to observe and articulate
The world I see
To create meaning through words
Creates connections through hurts
And brings unity to a world
Where previously it may not have been

It is an ever-evolving living organism
Mirroring styles and cultures of its time
It is the proof of a shared lived experience
Connecting us through our hearts
Our emotions
And our minds

Poetry is a responsibility
Manifesting a bridge across dimensions and
worlds
Existing partially on Earth and partially in the
celestial
Poetry is the translator of experiences that have
no words

And so to be a poet is a responsibility
To live with your eyes open
Speaking up when others would prefer you be
dumb
Because to be a poet is a responsibility
That comes as both a blessing and a curse

On Being

To Be Seen

I never needed stuff,
What I valued was your time.
I have faith in the universe
And its will to provide.

I don't need
Material
Gifts,
I
Am
Enough.
The greatest present
Is in your presence
And to know I am remembered
When I am gone.

The greatest gift
Is in the smallest symbols
That say
You are loved
You are thought of
And that you have indeed,
Been, Seen.

Sombre or Serene

Is existence destined to be melancholic?
Based on the separation of self
From the totality of light?
Or is it a grace
Untenable
Given the limitations of earthly human sight?

The beauty I behold leaves me
Trembling with anticipation
But the messages I've received Seem lost in
your translation.

I struggle with communication
Perceiving the world as I do,
Where you see sombre
I see so much more than the sadness you seem
to.

But it takes more than other people
To stop us from feeling this isolation.
Surrounded by defiance
Of accountability
Personal self-reflection.

Blind to the beauty
Offered up by Mother Nature,

It's our perception that deciphers
The perfection Gaia gave us.

A spider's web
For example,
As representation of a perfect creation.
A home
Or a trap,
Depending on your interpretation.

There is beauty
In the tragedy
Depending on whether you are the food
Or the fed
Or on if you believe that each fly's journey ends
There
Helpless
Trapped on a web.

Who triumphs here,
The spider or the fly?
Depends on the next part of this journey
And in what you believe happens
To the metaphysical spirit
After our earthly bodies die.
Whose experience in this scene allows for the
most growth
The physical nutrition received
Or the transmutation in the unknown?

Change happens when you reframe your experience
And see the pain undergone is no more than a teacher,
Evolving humanity over a billion years from
Where it first started
As a single cell amoeba.

Your attachments to earthly experiences
Are your biggest obstacles to overcome.
Freedom comes from surrendering
To the will of the universe
And allowing yourself
To experience
The journeys that you are on.

Our souls observed themselves into consciousness
And through these human experiences they
Continue to grow.
So, for me, our body's death is no more sombre
Than the decaying cocoon
A caterpillar outgrows.

There may be sadness in the separation
Where souls have formed earthly bonds
But time as we all know it now
Will seem like only moments that they were gone.

Symmetry is only possible
With enough distance from scene,
A butterfly's wing might look like chaos
Until you step back and are able to see its
spread wings.

But I am nobody's champion
And strive only in competition with myself.
The limitations of my communications
Compounded only by the limitations I place on
myself.

Blessed with night vision
Because I have lived in the dark
And I know now,
Only by keeping your eyes open
Do you get to see colours start to spark.

I want to live in a kinder world but
fundamentally that starts with me.
It has to start with me because my reality is just
a reflection of the person I choose to be.

Our individual truths are only ever based on a
personal nostalgia
So beware of anyone who will tell you their
opinion is more than conjecture.

We enter into this life to experience,

Not comprehend it.
The red pills just another avoidant tactic
For the journeys
Our souls were intended.

Because only when you free yourself from fear
And surrender without attaching labels
Does your life start to emerge
With possibilities that are endless.

I spread what I see as beauty
Your interpretation is a mirror to your soul.
What you see as sombre
I see as serene,
When seen as a whole.

So, is our existence
Destined to be melancholic
When we are all just crests of a wave,
Returning to the ocean
From where we were first made?

I crafted these words like I was crafting a map,
So that when you find them and hear them,
You too can find your way back.

Gratitude

You can never understand the darkness
Until someone turns on the lights.
You cannot describe the dawn,
To someone who has only ever lived at night.
You cannot comprehend the enormity
With eyes that only see in parts.
We cannot understand our purpose
Till the obstacles are moved from our purpose's
path.

So, if in fact I chose this life
Or if, in fact, this life chose me,
I accept with faith and humility,
The gifts this life has bestowed,
Graciously.

In Between

There is you,
And there is me
And in between there are the lies we tell
ourselves
To navigate through the maze of deceit
Constructed in this make-believe reality
We created to make ourselves feel
As though we understand some part of
That which we perceive.

Trying to survive by adapting to those who
surround us.
Suffocating authenticity
Or originality
For fear of standing out.

Murdering emotions cast from anyone
unaccounted for,
While my heart bleeds for someone to notice
me Inside this cocoon I am too afraid to leave.

But the ramblings of a mad woman hold no
weight in a litigious society
Run by men,
For men,
For the men,
Who make the cut.

Mesmerised and moulded
By the misogynistic malignant myopathy making
a mockery out of the men who refuse to
conform to an archaic notion of masculinity.
For they,
And we,
Are the ones who will reap the repeated regrets
of such calamitous remorse.
Rolling around this rung out regime,
Ruling the masses into rigid conformity.

For I am who I am!
Descending from the mountain like Moses with
the tablets,
This is my burden to carry,
Through my doubts and my insecurities.

For I am all of my strengths
And all of my flaws,
No more,
But no less!
And I reject the shame I inherited from your
curse.

I will not be silenced.
Sa Ta Na Ma
'Truth is my guide'
I am the guide
As I am the guided.

Blinded bewildered bemused
Longing for a clarity of vision uniting all divisions
Previously keeping us apart.
Craving unity.
Seeking totality.
On a mission,
Till we all accept a vision that see's more than
sight.

On the wisdom based on a nostalgia you nurse,
We are all just mirrors of our greatest
achievements and our most overbearing
remorse.
We are all constrained by an inherent set of
rules,
Imprisoned without cages,
Our jailers live inside us
All we have to do is scream, 'fuck you!'
But no one dares
Because I am he
And ultimately, he is you.
Nursing the same fears And the same truths.
It is all within our control
But in truth
There is safety in the walls confining you.

There is breath
And there is stillness

And in between there is the universe
Peaking back at you,
In those moments you throw away like garbage
As she reaches out
Longing for communication,
Never giving up hope
That you will find her truth...
Everything you need
Is already within each one of you.

Hell Has a Nightlight

Born in a bedroom drawer,
The last regret of a teenage runaway
Too naive to believe
That adding babies
Doesn't always make
For happy families.

Too small for a cot
They packed her up with their clothes
And their socks
To stop their new toy from rolling away.
But clothes and socks soon became cruel words
And locks.

But in the darkness
She found
A nightlight
To guide her way.

Exotic romances from far travelled strangers
might seem like the start of a fairy tale...
To some.
But childish dreams of kings and queens
Can quickly turn to nightmarish scenes
With two jobs and screaming baby
Crammed into a bedsit for one.

But flowers that grow in the shade
Grow wild
And
Unconventionally.
Observing the light with more curiosity

Than flowers that grow
With a sense of
More
Normality.

And her spirit soared,
Like wildfire
Uncontrollably ablaze
Releasing a phoenix
No terror could keep caged
And she wrote.
In the hope that someone would hear.
Because no one would listen to what a child had
to say.
She put all the words on paper,
With dreams of a saviour,
Never conceiving that that saviour was always
within.

She fell asleep in the shadows
And woke up in the light,
Having confronted her own darkness
The light shone twice as bright.

But just like a seed that grows into a plant
The transformation undergone
Began alone,
In the dark.

No miracle emerged
No thunderbolt struck
Yet by guidance and divinity
There was a path to be took.

These days, she spends a lot of her time arguing
with God,
It tends to be more of a one-sided debate but
she still gives it all that she's got.
Because she can be stubborn
But not by mistake,
It was infinite wisdom
That created the reliance it would take.

And when I talk of God
I reference divine femininity
And pray glory to the goddesses who rise each
morning
From the ashes of their own historic brutalities.

Because to be a survivor is to survive one day
To another,
Drawing strength from confronting the
experiences that were harder.

Knowing that the days that feel manageable are
often followed by days that feel darker,
But it's in the discovery of our purpose, we
create a life that is brighter.

And if I'm truly honest
My thoughts are still consumed by these tales.
And I wrestle
With the consequences
Of decisions once made.
But the battles to live
Is no longer battle disguised
Ashamed or embarrassed of the demons
That hide.

Because in the depths of that light,
Is where we become our own beacons,
In the strength of our resilience,
Where we unveil our own saviours.
In our compassion,
Exists the start of our own love affair,
And when we fall in love with ourselves
We reframe our existence here.

And even when those demons run rampage
through her brain,
She sleeps with the night light on
So she never loses her way.

To Believe

I believe that this world is terrifying
Whilst
At the same time
Being full of awe

That it can scare us
Into submission
To be broken and bitter.
But we have a choice.

A choice to cower.
To feel owed an apology by a life passing us by,
Without so much as a second thought.
Casting resentment from our place of sorrow
At anyone
Unafraid to rise above and soar.

Or

We can use that fear to drive us,
To push us.
And with that force
We can become anything we want.
I believe that
If we choose to accept this drive
We can excel and grow beyond our wildest
imagination.

I believe that the fundamental energies that
brought us here,
Brought us here for good.
I believe that everything,
However painful or incompressible to a mortal
mind,
Happens, in the long run, for that good.

I believe that the pain we individually
experience are lessons,
Not punishments,
That aid our growth and evolution.

I believe that our lives are deep with meaning.
I believe that nothing happens by chance.
That there is no such thing as coincidence
And that the people we meet
For good or bad
Were placed on our path by divine intervention
To aid us on a predestined journey that we
Ourselves
Chose.

I believe that the kindness I have received from
friends and strangers alike was placed in front of
me to help me make sense of the journey within
in order to extend the same back to those who
now struggle with the battles I once did.
I believe that I exist to love

To embody love in all its many
Forms
Without expectation or reciprocation.

I believe that the force that propels us
Hurtling through this incomprehensible reality,
Will make sense only when we have the
capacity to understand.

I believe that I and I alone am responsible for
my choices.
I must be the one to make them.
I must be able to live with them.
And I must be able to live with their
consequences.

I believe that the difference between us all is in
knowing the fear
But taking a chance anyway.
And I believe that I have lived my life having
nothing to regret.

On Observation
Tales from the 65

This is a story about two little girls
Who caught the no 65 bus to school
Together
For 5 years.
Rolled up skirts and over the knee socks,
Strangers to independence
They carved identities out of their uniforms
And that precious time.

Searching for a sense of their
Adolescence,
The journey was more
Than a route from A to B,
It was a portal to a forbidden world.
Taking risks
It's hard to remember you're a naive child
When you know things 15 year olds shouldn't
know.

Too afraid to be angry.
Avoiding the curse of frustration and collapse,
Bitterness and loss.
Parentified children, parenting their parents
Never accepting
Always rebelling

Oblivious to costs.
For 5 years they waited for that bus.
Headlights approaching like a beacon of hope
through rain, sleet and fog
And set sail on their daily voyage of mayhem
and intrigue
Engaging willingly with anyone who would
entertain them.

The characters they meet, inhaled like oxygen
The stories they'd collect, their life rings.
No secret garden but a secret world where
those de pressed souls could soar.
Nurtured on the thrill this daily glimpse of
freedom exposed,
Encouraging each other to let their souls burst
free and become the people they now know.

For two little girls
Suffocating in an environment unable to hear
their needs
This daily adventure provided the capacity to
imagine
A different way of living could be achieved.
For most people the journey to school's
uneventful
But for these, it offered air to breathe.

Hindsight could make it seem silly or childish,
Though it was anything but.
It was a drive to survive.

I wonder if the bus driver knew he drove more
than a bus?

Wild

A long time ago
We played 40/40 on Vere Island
Tripping the light fantastic
On Dartmoor's finest mushrooms
Marinated in Buckfast wine
And childish idealism

We sat in a lemon-yellow kitchen
Covered in cigarette butts
And empty beer cans
Discussing Nietzsche and Darwin
And never saw the hypocrisy of our truths

We ate out of the Sainsbury's skip
Spending our money popping pills like smarties
Vomiting rainbows in the corner basin sink
Of some new best friend
We'd made only that night

We made love in sunken green gardens
Alive with ghost stories
Of tormented ancient spirits
Peering down on us
From the lead piped glass windows of
Dartington hall

We threw illegal parties in car parks

And danced waist deep in moorland lakes
High on ecstasy
And the hypnotic repetition of the 4:4

We climbed up onto roofs
Conducting ballet in the rafters

And danced through the dawn
Long into the day

We rushed across stages
At events we didn't belong at
Riding piggyback
Pumping a fist to an imaginary gabba beat

We got chased out by bouncers
Pulling at our hair as they kicked us in the ribs
Discarded out into the wild
Left to hitch home from tie dyed passers by
Unsure whether it was OK to laugh at the abuse
we gave each other
And anyone else who tried to understand
Our morbid sense of camaraderie

We sat on staircases outside of parties we had
spent months before planning
Talking over each other and

Creating bonds that resonated deeper than the
bass line rattling through the windows from
inside

Dreadlocks and baggy trousers
Clothes covered in petrol and mud
Syphoning tanks
Anytime the music would stop

Because nothing could stop us
No laws
No finances
No heartbreak
Broken Records
Broken Bones
Broken Sanity
Nothing would stop us

We chased the lizard over the moon
Staring through the looking glass
And drinking Alice's magic potion
Only to lose ourselves down a rabbit hole
We ourselves had created

We descended in
And out
Of a madness we accepted as our normality
Never questioning the life we had come to know

We fell off of scaffolding
Asleep under cars and
In and out of love with each other
Only to come crashing down on top of each
other
When the music
Finally
Stopped.

We were more than friends
We were a reflection of each other
With the naivety of youth to believe
That it would never end

So much so
We didn't even think to say goodbye when it did

We were the freedom
To make mistakes
And we relished in making them
We were the wild people write stories about
And we were happy,
But that was a long time ago.

Perfect

Wake up..
Meditate
Eat healthily.
Walk dogs.

Write a report, meditate, eat healthy, don't
snack!
Send emails, clean the kitchen, pay the bills,
Respond in a timely manner to friends...
Date!

Make an effort, get involved, put yourself out
there!
You can't just sit back and hope for the best!
Sleep
Sleep early
Sleep well.
Sleep through the night
Wake up
Wake up early,
Be productive in the mornings, wake up right!

Repeat.

Be happy
Be professional
Be educated

Be successful, be financially secure!
Be well read
Be creative
Be interesting
Be thoughtful Be aware!
Be kind!
Eat right, don't be too thin don't be too thick!
Be sexy
Be funny
Be a good lover
Be accessible
Be a friend
Be a mother...

Be perfect!
Wake up.
Wake up!
Wake up!!!

I have a secret
I am not perfect
And the pressure to pretend to be
Is suffocating.

Social media sits on its bench
Casting judgments
From a gallery
Safely protected behind a one-way screen
Avoiding the ugliness of their own reflection.

Fighting for a front row seat,
Excited with their knitting
Hungry for the beheading
Of the latest casualty of war,
Highlighting flaws and mistakes
To an ungracious audience
Ready with matches
To set fire to the sacrificial pyre.

I am not perfect
And to be honest I'm not convinced I was ever
fooling anyone
With my clever masquerades
Anyway.
Criticising myself for getting bigger
For feeling dumber
For falling short of my own expectations

Because I should have gotten up earlier
I should have tried harder
I should have known better than to be a human
being Who sometimes makes mistakes.

And after all
What does it mean to be perfect?
And to be good enough for who?
For ourselves?
Or in the eyes of those who find it their place to
judge?

Carefully avoiding walking past any mirrors that
might reflect imperfections of their own.
And why would you want to be perfect?
When true beauty exists in the imperfections
that we learn to own.
In the cracks,
In the asymmetry,
In the vulnerabilities we seek the strength to be
brave enough to show.

No! I am not perfect
I am not always happy
And I don't always say the things I want to say in
the right way.
I struggle with my mental health
I leave my work till the last minute
And I don't look like my Instagram pictures most
days.
I don't balance my cheque book
Or drink 8 glasses of water
Or manage 5 fruits and veg in an average day.
I run away from healthy relationships
Then complain I can't meet anyone
And I emotionally overeat to compensate.
I rarely shop local,
I hoard material possessions
And I don't always wash up straight away.

Because I am not perfect
And I end up judging myself worse than anyone
else has the time to
Then I eat my feelings,
Drowning in a veil of my own shame.
Because I am not perfect
And trying to pretend to has been killing me
So... I'm done!
I'm done pretending!
To be perfect....
At least, I am... for today!

Parallel Lives

We live in parallel units
On top of each other
N' side by side,
Creating symbiotic existences
For our meaningless lives.

We fall prey to defences
Too shrouded to see
That the only people we hurt
Are ourselves
Eventually.

We are hopeless and hopeful
In the goals that we set
While trampling on each other
Without remorse or regret.

But in the end, there's no difference
In what we all get.
Hostage to the belief that we're owed
Something still better yet.

We live side by side
In our meaningless lives,
Creating our dramas
To hide
The torment inside.

We live upside down
Back to front
And inside out,
Waiting for someone to hand us a key
That we've already got.

Disposable

Enraptured by the ephemeral beauty
Of what you know,
Can never last.

Elipsed by the transience,
Eclipsing your hearts desire
To mend
What was broken in your past

But this disposable culture
Makes a mockery of permanence.
When forever means,
Until something better comes along.

Exposing the vultures,
Ready to tear at the parts
This festering wound continues to feast upon.

They come and they go
Like fashion or flying ants or fleas,
Feeding off your emotions
And feelings
For the things that you have seen.

Vocal with disdain
And rage for what you've known.

Till you become another broken thing
Easier disposed of
Than nurtured or fixed whole.

Too much value is placed on that which cannot
last.
Relationships built upon the superficial
Lack foundations
To withstand
The impacts of stormy weather
Or emotional blasts.

Land masses filled with plastic,
empty promises and what could have beens.
Pilgrimages to the disposable nature
Of our modern hopes and dreams.

Still, we gather fervently
Squirrelling away our acorns to get us through
sudden droughts of self-esteem.
As though their containment
Can contain the loneliness a person ultimately
feels.
One more upon one more upon one more we
grow
Finding our worth in the envy of others
Rather than in how much compassion we
extend or show.
 Hoarding material possessions to

Camouflage just how insignificant we really are.
Kings of the junkyards.
Queens of the beauty parlour.
Glittering externally
To avoid how empty our meaningless lives feel
from afar.

Still, we are teased by the haunting memories
Of a perfect past.
Eclipsing any desires
To build a foundation
On something that could now last.

But only in our memories
Do dreams ever really come true.
Clinging to the fantasies
Blinkered to the realities
Of that life that you knew.

A Letter to the Disenfranchised Youth

My letter to the disenfranchised youth
Who tell me that they don't believe in politics.
They find no interested in old men debating old
laws
And considering policies by which our society
could rise
Or
Fall!

Your apathy fills me with despair!
Politics is the conversation by which conclusions
are reached pertaining to the conduct of those
bound to it
And if you are not bound to the conversation,
How can you expect
Inclusion in its conclusion!

If, like Nietzsche, you believe life is to suffer,
To suffer without cause
Just makes a mockery of it all.

The wonder of this world exists inside
Our ability to walk the line between fearing the
ephemeral and risking everything,
For
Something!

To discover your truth worth dying for is what
can make the difference between existing
And
Living!
So why would you exist just to suffer when you
can live
In a world
Full of wonder?

My message to the disenfranchised youth
Your anger is a gift
Channel it and change that which makes you
mad.

You will never have as much energy and passion
as you do today.
Time moves on even when we don't,
Bringing with it apathy and exhaustion.

Anger left unfocused will only add a resentful
bitterness to your nostalgia.
Regret nothing.

Be the change you long for

Because we're British (AKA The Butchers Apron)

(Inspired by '52 Times Britain was a Bell End' by J Felton)

We stand on one side of the escalator
With withering looks for those who don't know.
We butter our bread whatever the spread,
And call people weird when they don't.
We cannot avoid an orderly queue,
Unafraid to chastise anyone who cuts in.
And laugh about how Brits abroad
Can be 'so embarrassing.'

We like to feel the burden,
Working longer hours than the E.U.
And spend our days complaining about the weather,
As though the weather were something new.

We cannot agree on our politics,
Prefer a cheeky smile to considered policies.
And condemn creativity and culture,
As paganism and heresy.

Our museums are akin to police crime units
Holding the evidence of our thievery,

While we protect ourselves,
And change the law
To make it illegal to do the moral thing.

We treat our dogs better than most people,
At least better than the refugees we 'graciously'
allow in.
Rushing home in time for 'stenders
Rather than educate ourselves on the journey's
that they have been.

We are independently responsible for more
deaths
Than any nation has ever been.
As we bolster 'no surrender!'
Awarding ourselves the heroes of history.

We drink more tea than China
Having traded it 'fairly' for our home-grown
opium.
While we sent our starving out to the colonies
Labelling them murderers and criminals.

We rebranded our slaves,
Calling them 'apprentices,'
Forced to work 40hrs a week for naught.
Then congratulated ourselves on being more
'educated'
Than the 'savages' that we had bought.

We called our crusades 'missions of mercy'
And not the barbaric acts of terrorism that
they'd actually been.
In the narcissistic belief that we knew better.
And that our God would defend such horror
scenes.

We traded countries we swore to protect,
Like collectors' items or novelty cards,
Invaded nations exposed to neglect
And introduced homophobia and misogyny
worldwide.

But no sex please,
We're British!
We don't talk about such things,
We keep it all
Behind closed doors
To protect the empire's
Greatest sins.

No sex please.. we're British!
We can't be blamed for what our ancestors did!
Although we can take credit
For any good we've Inherited
Without graciously acknowledging.

So perhaps we could afford to be a little less British,
In our rush to steal, trample or take credit for everything,
Because I would love to be able to be proud to be British,
If we could show some accountability of our historic sins.

Two Voices

There are two voices in my head
And they are both me.
One who represents my more human side,
And chatters away incessantly.

The other resonates in a celestial tone
And communicates implicitly.
She is more of is a gentle knowing
Than her counterpart's commentary.

Often referred to as intuition
She's that internal flutter the stillness exposes.
A vibrational understanding
Holding up my mirror wherever I go

She's sometimes harder to hear.
Sometimes harder to know.
But when you turn down the distractions
The truth is plainly clear.

I hear her whispers gently
In my struggles with the light
Even if it's the harder option
You'll always know which option's right.

Lessons in Compassion

Our lessons
As with our journeys
Are all individual
And unique,
Compassion for the struggle's others'
experiences
Deserves discretion
When we speak.

What may seem like an excuse to one
Could be another's greatest affliction,
When life presents as a series of hurdles and
contradictions.
You are where you are on your journey
By a combination of being blessed as well as
strong,
So spare judgement for another's reality
And the path that they are on.

Though your mountain may be high
And your struggle may be real,
You can never truly comprehend the obstacles
Another feels.

Though your vision may be clear
And empathy sincere

To bare humility through frustration
We could all try harder to adhere.

No one can ever truly understand the
mountains a person's climbed
Or what sorrow lies behind the
Happy smiles and 'I'm fines!.'
We are all tormented from cradle to the grave
In our battle to understand that
Which cannot be man-made.

But as protection,
We project that of ourselves which we cannot
bear,
Onto the face of another
And deflect our criticisms there.

So ultimately in compassion for those you've
now assigned fault,
Is in fact self-compassion for those same parts
in you,
The same parts that you forgot.

For the same parts you've resisted and despise,
The same parts you would do anything to black
out and hide,
The same parts that keep holding you back,
The same parts you project when feeling low or
attacked.

Those same parts are the prison of your making,
Those same parts are what will feed your
contempt
And complacency.

Those same parts are your battles to overcome
If you choose to live this life emancipated of
what's already done.

But our lessons,
As with our journeys,
Are all individual
And unique,
And finding compassion for our ourselves can
make the more vulnerable among us
Feel weak.

But in the understanding of these contradictions
and they hurdles that they present
Is what can untimely free us
From living a life that we resent.

Tragic Beautiful

I find myself obsessed with the beauty in the
tragic.
In observing the demise of everything blessed
with life.
Of the poetry that is offered to us
Yet ignored by most,
In terror of their own inevitable goodnight.

I catch myself in the grasp of the decaying,
Willing life into an elusive,
Yet
Taunting love.

Transfixed by the beauty of the discarded,
Tossed away like garbage,
Carrying it away like kisses on a breeze.

Lost and longing,
The lingering breath
Inhale, exhale
Like the final moments on your final cigarette.

Floating away with it the hopes,
Riding the waves of the tide.
Released from the restraints and prisons
Of those man-made ties that bind

Whatever Happened to the Milkman?

I unsubscribe
To this glossed over
Super filtered
Size zero
High definition
Finger pointing
Unforgiving
Template
Dictating who we are supposed to be.
It's all too shiny
Too mass produced
Over produced
The records lost its groove.

Whatever happened to the milkman?
What happened to kids playing conkers in the
street?
Whatever happened to knowing your
neighbours?
And running home with grazes on your knee?

Whatever happened to Saturday morning
television?
What happened to riding bikes up and down the
street?
Whatever happened to waving 'morning'
To the those now invisible

As we swipe left and right
On telephone screens?

We were wild!
Mindless with abandon
Chasing laughter
As laughter chased me

We were unafraid
The last children of the milk-float
We didn't know how lucky we had been!

Whatever happened to the milkman?
In that simpler time before technology.
Could we ever have imagined,
Just how alien the future was going to be?

Did we ever say thank you to the milkman?
Or wave goodbye as the cart evaporated down
the street,
Whirling away with it the remnants,
Of all what was to become a distant memory.

How old are you?

How old are you?
Not your years of life
Or the number of birthday celebrations
That you have had
But how old is your soul?
How old are the eyes
That make sense of this world you know?

There's a place of balance
Where living and loving can co-exist.
Where they can develop in a harmony
That brings a joy to those who don't resist.

It's the place between youthful naivety
And knowing resentment.
It not a birth right
It's not a free download with every birthday
cake.

It comes from an internal growing that you
cannot cheat,
Buy or imitate.
It comes from facing the mirror and being ok
with what looks back.
It comes from staying with the grief,
When the grief starts to crack.
It comes from being OK with your faults

Even when people throw them at you in shame.
It comes from knowing it's ok to be different,
And that comparing is a losing game.

It comes from holding it together when all you
want to do is let it go.
It comes from co existing with your fears
Accepting your sadness
And your tears.
Even when you despise them
And the reason they have such a hold.
Letting them wash over you
And re-emerging
In a more confident, accepting way.

How old are you?
How old is your soul?
How many years have you lived?
With that voice in control?
How old is your heart?
Is it crippled by your head?
Does it love with abandon?
Or fear intimacy instead?

How old are you?
And how can you know?
Till you silence all that's been taught to you
And relearn the truth you've always known.

The Beach

Watching families congregate along the beach.
So casually
So naturally
As though it was the simplest thing to see.

Playing with their children.
Smiling,
Laughing,
Getting mucky,

No forced endeavour,
No exhaustion,
Just effortless glee

Curiosity intrigues me
Who each of them are?
Where did they meet?
How have they created a life that has always
alluded me
So
Seemingly,
Easily?

Is it all an illusion,
Or was it just their destiny

Perhaps they have all been told a secret
That everyone's kept
Deceitfully.

I find myself frozen by a moment
That triggers fear internally.
But the family laugh so casually
I realise why this life was never meant for me.

I watch an older couple
Walk together
Hand in hand.
Then stop along the ocean
To do their stretches in the sand.
So supple,
So flexible
So connected to each other in ways I may never
understand.

They fall into a routine
Without words
Without instruction.

I wonder are they lovers
Who met later on in life?
Or have they been together
Through years of trouble and strife?

They finish off their stretches and walk off
Silently.
No words are spoken
No tension
No grief.

How can something so natural
So seemingly easy for everyone else,
Be such a mystery
That so difficult to get?

How can such a pleasure
Such a simple delight
Be the only thing in this universe
That's just so hard to get right.

Cairo

My eyes open against the rattling window of an
old rusty bus
With a brown no 7 written in a circle on the
side.
It's funny to push people away when you're so
lonely.

I watch fixated
As a city slowly emerges out of the desert
landscape,
Like an old silent movie,
Playing in the rear-view mirror,
Hanging precariously off the passenger side
window.

A shop, some billboard, a sudden sprawling
metropolis of half-finished buildings and
intertwining roads.
Alive to a chorus of black and white taxis and
dirty old cars.
That sudden noise of the city is jarring.

Between the buildings and billboards Flash the
tops of three ancient wonders,
Glorious and proud.
Reminding everyone why Cairo is more than a
failed

Homage to a western Mecca
Most people here love
To despise.

Inside the city wall
Her crowded streets illuminate the isolation.
I feel it more
The more people there are around.

Dusty roads with shops selling empty bird cages
And baskets woven by hand.
Men smoking shishas and playing dice
Before the calls to prayer echo through the
streets.
I imagine that this life's superior to the Babylon
I've come to know.

Still, I choose to hide myself in clouds.

14 million vehicles.
The roads speak the language of the horn.
From minibuses to tuk tuks to old rusty trucks
with people sitting casually on the top.
Driving here is like playing a game of Tetris
Except here
You lose,
And people die.

We drive past pile ups of trucks and cars
Desensitised

Women with boxes on their heads
And moped carrying full families
Babies in their arms
No helmets.
Men carrying trays full of foods and baked
breads.
Tall men in galabeyas and angry women
shouting 'Imshi,
Yuhrubetic!'
Waving their slippers at young boys
Staring at my yellow hair
And I wonder, where do I even belong?

It's been so long.

The sun sets behind a smog ridden sky
Lighting it up like America on the 4th of July
And its city lights start to twinkle
One by one.

But this is a city that doesn't sleep
The night air brings reprieve from the days
blistering heat
Seeing more people out onto its streets and
The sound of song and laughter start to fill the
evening air.

And it's not like I know these streets or that they
were ever safe for me to roam.
I don't speak the language they speak
In attitude or tongue.
The pain of being here has always outweighed
any joy I could have ever known
And Cairo is not a place that could have ever
called home.

But we share blood
And doesn't that count for something?
Centuries of secrets gifted us with grace and
knowledge
With mystical prophecies
And historic solace.
For the wisdom that's trodden through this dust
before me
Seeps and secretes
Into me.

Oh Cairo, what pleasure have you known?

Thieves steal what was never theirs.
Collateral damage of the thrill
The sins they bear.
But in my search for an escape route
I never thought about what was taken,
I just looked for sanctuary
And my ancestry became the trade off.

But in Cairo there is more than the brutality of a
past There is a history denied

I wonder what would change if the truth was
known.
I turn my back.
Do they judge me?
Or envy me?
Is there even a line between?

The women here are tough.
Raised by a city that has taught them how to
survive.
Smiles hide sins men don't try disguise
While women cower their light
And continue to live a patriarchal lie
All in the name of a regime they long ago gave
up hope in.

But fear controls
Tougher than any weapon or military coop.
50 years of a dictatorship
Crumbling
Like rotten cheese,
While the walls announce
The rise of the inquisitive youth.
The words,
'If your government shuts down your internet
Shut down your government'

Scrawled in red paint on the side.
Perhaps change is afoot.

But Cairo doesn't cry.
We share our secret
Her and I.
She sheds no tears for her past
No rain she cries.
She glistens with the jewels the Nile supplies,
Pulsating her heartbeat through her desert
lands,
Feeding her
20 million people
She'll never tell,
She never cries.

I wonder what my grandmother would have
made of me.
A woman I never knew who's
Influence has trickled down like ever decreasing
circles,
Affecting the lives of three women she could
have never of imagined.
I denied these parts of me for so long.
The diamonds in the dirt.
A humanity trapped in hell.
Why did I never think about what was stolen
from me?

Why...
Why did I never tell?

The remnant of ancestral trauma slips through
the hands of time
Like the deserts sands
That once belonged to City's
Histories
Forgot.

But while the blood of my ancestors still dances
in the Nile,
She offers strength from hers, to hers, to mine.

In the hands of three women stood a choice
Now with this generation
It dies.
And maybe it's just time.

What else is there to say when there are no
more words
left to let go of.

Not all weight carried is worth it.
Not all that glitters is gold.
Not all lying in the dust is worthless
Not all stories are destined to be told
These women got tired.

But these women don't cry.
They wave their slippers and ululate.

We learned from a city what it was to survive.

Religion Stole My Relationship with God

I never lost my faith in God
I lost my faith in religion
In the installation of division
Enforcing this very human condition
Perpetuating separation and collision
Through a man-made narration,
Created purely for the purpose of
Twisting blessed infinite wisdom
To serve masters of greed and control
Suiting specific individuals
Turning wine into water
The fed into the hungry
Beauty into sin
Unity into division

The very opposite of divine intention

I lost my faith in man

I never lost by faith in God
I lost my faith in the representation
Being communicated and translated.
In an autocracy with cruel expression
Hiding behind Gods name to spread bile and
apprehension
Rejecting and deflating men who did not fit into
a projected expectation

Declaring war on love
Rather than extending its celebration to all of
Gods children
Who would pit one man against another man
because of the colour of a man's skin
Or because of who that man consensually loves
Or chooses to have a family with.
Simultaneously suppressing the divine feminine
Terrified of her celestial acceleration
Creating commodity out of virginities
Bought and sold under man's watchful
scrutinies

I lost my faith in its administration
In its manipulative inventions
Twisting historic knowledge from its origins
Like the lunar goddess sin.
Manufacturing servitudal conditioning
Stripping away creativity and expression
Aimed at raising elevations

Because it so much easier to maintain a
benumbed congregation

I lost my faith in the absurd suggestion
That killing children in the name of God
Was ever blessed appellation
That the acquisition of land and power could
ever be behind divine designation.

In the notion that favourable acceptance would
be given to those with a regular physical
attendance
Over acknowledging the beauty in individual
elation

I lost my faith in an environment
That would use Gods name to justify its
violence.
Offering salvation in return for obedient
compliance.
In the disparity between
Loving universality and septic
contemptuousness,
Feeding misinformation on a regular basis.
Focussing on differences
Rather than on the wonders uniting us

I lost my faith to belong

Born into this world screaming
Ripped from more than our mothers' wombs.
Sorrow hits us in the solar plexus
A metaphysical kick in the guts
But our Sacral Chakra's
Are grounded in Muladhara
Raising Kundalini
Red, Orange, Yellow, Green, Blue
Where I found the voice to speak

And rise like a phoenix from the ashes of the
memory
They would have kept from me.
Indigo, Violet
Radiating
Like a path in front of me,
Returning me to clarity

My vision cleared
I found my way home

I never lost my faith in science
I lost my faith in its lectured bias
In its lack of humility
Despite its infallible history
Demonstrating repeatedly
That just because you cannot prove something
Does not mean that its wrong
It's that immovable rigidity that
Throughout history
Would again and again
Trip itself up
Such a lack of curiosity
Would have us all continuing to believe that the
world was still flat
And that Galileo was still wrong

I never lost my faith in love
I lost my faith in its truthful acquisition

In a world now subject to deception
Forever searching for reconnection
Destined to perpetuate this unsatiated rejection
Distracted by superficial projections
Stopping us from asking too many questions.

The taboo of flesh creates shameful obsessions
Such a useful distraction

I lost my faith in motive

I never lost my faith in God
I never lost my faith in the beauty being offered
us
I never lost my faith in trees
In the cool night air or
In a warm summer breeze
I never doubted for a moment that the green
would return when winter took its leave
I never lost my faith in the sun rise
And that the moon would once again fill the
nights sky's
I never lost my faith that gravity would never let
me go
Or that the universe would always know what
was best for my ever-growing soul
I never lost my faith in divine intent
Or that we would all ultimately be guided by
what was best for human ascent.

Despite their best efforts to create confusion to
this end
By those sworn to defend
Despite this

I never lost my faith in God

That's Not How I Spell Love

They say that love happens when you least
expect it
That it usually comes when you're looking the
other way.
And when it comes,
It come with such ferocity
It causes chaos to your health, work and play.

But that doesn't look like love to me,
That's not something I have any desire to be.
For me love is in the everyday
In the people
Who surround me's
Little loving ways.
And the most beautiful kind of love to see
Was when I learned to appreciate the love living
right in front of me.

They say that love can make you crazy
That it can make you lose your mind.
Drives us nuts ruminating with obsession
And cause our hearts to be painfully tried.

But that doesn't feel like love to me.
That feels more like a deep-rooted fear of
intimacy.
Because the sweetest love that I ever knew

Was the one beside me encouraging me to grow.
And when you learn to stop pushing that love away
You find the one you've longed for was always here to stay.

They say that true love is hard to find
And I think that's true for the emotional blind,
Telling tales about how one day your prince will come
And how a girl must wait patiently until he does.

But fairy tales have no place in reality
Because that's not how I spell love
Or where love should ultimately be.
Because the happiest love I happened to see,
Was the peace in the mirror
Looking back
Contently
At me

On Love, Lust and Co-dependency

Consent

Angels never sang a sweeter song.
I can't concentrate when he looks up at me and
smiles that sly Corner of the mouth smile
Like he knows what's going on.
 If he's psychic
I'm in so much trouble.
He's shy
Struggles with eye contact for too long.
So, looks away
Keeps his hat down low
But he can't help but look back up
To see if I'm
Still Looking.

Now he definitely knows.

I struggle to articulate myself when he sits so
close,
He smells like fresh linen and my next mistake.

My thighs tense as he leans in and laughs.
I match his laughter
Like I'm so casual

But all I can think about are his hands and what they might feel like if they came into contact with my skin.

With a body so sweet
It had to be made by the devil
Because
God knows
Only Lucifer could create something
So delicious.
It had to be
Bad
For me.

He stays and walks me hand in hand through our history and traumas,
Patiently looking for black holes to deliver us from a past that's even darker
And enter a future we are both afraid to grace.

What use is love when your leaving is as inevitable as tragedy?

But hair without knots in it
Is not as satisfying to run your fingers through as hair with the odd tangle.
And I bring a head full of many tangles.

But is it too many?

Vibrations seep out of him like radiation out of a
damaged hazmat suit.
Filling the room with his aura
And oh, I want to believe.

We take it in turns to cry.
And I fall,
Hard.

If my heart were as big as Jupiter,
In this moment
I couldn't love him more.

I can't breathe when he touches me like that
Leans into my neck seeking consent.
Mutual exploration
Ultimately so much more satisfying than
Seeking
Solo
Delectation

It's that simplicity of exchange,
That creates Change.
Igniting a chain reaction

Touch becomes a thing I have never
experienced
And it's all I can do not to beg,
For more.

He places the flesh on his lips against my lips
And inhales
Like he's bracing himself for what's to come.
Before landing his Kiss
So gently.
Like he's handling papyrus
Savouring the moment with all the reverence
such treasures become.

His second kiss lands harder and takes my
breath away
The room Trembles,
Or is it me?

He cinches me in at the waist,
Handling the cascading mess of hair draped
across my neck
Demonstrating intimacy my fears would usually
reject

Once again, his hands are all I can think about
But now his touch is all I can feel.

In the strength to show true vulnerability
Lay secrets,
That opened more than doors.

Our heartbeats pressed into the divine
Vibrations rising from root to crown,

Coronating him my King
And me his Queen

Battlelines concede

Trust reinstated where Love
Should have always Been

Kisses

Kisses outside a train station
Or in an airport lounge
A reflection of hope
Pressed on lips from lips
A touch that creates wings
And halos
And perfect endings
Or beginnings
Of films.

Kisses outside a train station, Give meaning to
life.

A Co-dependent Love Story
Intro by W.H.Mearns

"As I was walking up the stairs
I met a man who wasn't there
He wasn't there again today
I wish that he would go away"

We met when we were barely more than
children,
Playing dress up
In a real-life Wendy house
On an old
Cobbled street,
Brimming with brightly coloured characters
And houses straight off the set of pigeon street.

Just a little boy
And a little girl
Trying to get it right
In a make-believe fantasy masquerading as a
life.

He wore what looked like a badly fitted costume
jacket and had dirty blonde dreadlocks
Which in combination made me think of Fagan.

Hard to imagine now that he was such a college
heart throb.

Cock sure and undeterred by consequence
He somehow convinced you to feel special
But more than that,
He convinced you that you were special.
That when he was talking to you
You were the only one he wanted to be talking
to,
Whilst all the while knowing,
He could never truly care about anyone
But himself.

But to exist between those two places
Was exhilarating,
Like a drug high no synthetic substitute could
replicate
And I,
I am an addict!

I danced in the chaos,
Wild with the chase!
Embraced the familiarity
Having never known love in any other way.

Colluding with the illusion
That I didn't care,

All the time caring so much
I died a little everyday
Till all that was left
Was a shadow of the girl he'd first met
Desperate for the drug now offered less and
less.

Till one day
He lay looked up,
Naked and empty handed and said,
"Well, what did you expect?"

It's said that expectation is the root of all
misery,
And after a lifetime of chasing what I knew he
could never give me,
I died that final death.
But he had never lied.
I'd known right from the start.
So, who did I have to blame for ever offering
him my heart?

A lifetime of rented accommodations
And 25 years later we uncovered lives apart.
Tiptoeing out from under the weight of each
other's shadow,
Like wounded animals,
Nursing bruised egos

And a wretched comedown from the brutal
realisation that we could no longer blame our
unhappiness on each other,
Under that mystical guise of love,
Anymore.
Beaten and broken by a lifetime of pretending
not to see each other's needs,
But as we never learned how to put on our own
gas masks on,
We'd never learned how to help each other
breathe.

He once asked me "I'm here, is that not
enough?"
Physically here but emotionally nowhere.
We both may as well have both been nowhere.

Ceasing to exist
Passing on the stairs
Ghosts in our own lives
Clinging to the memory
Of that magic that once surrounded a little boy
And a little girl,
Failing to get it right
On that funny old, cobbled street
In that other place, In that other life.

She Can't Be Me

Time
Is never time enough
When a dream is over
And you have to watch them
Fall asleep
To the dreams of someone new.

Laughing at the jokes you once told me
When no one else existed
Inside this reverie.
When love songs were created in the shade of
your gaze.

Juvenile fantasy's innocent hearts crave.

But, I see you,
And I know..
She can't be me,
Any more than he can be you.

Saturated in each other
Till we rung each other dry.
Plastering over the cracks with naive sentiments
such as,
'Love will conquer all"
And
'All you need is love'.

Finger food of loves fool
Just a collection of stardust cosmically attached
Bewitched into believing we were the centre of
the universe.
Unable to acknowledge the truth.
We were just the centre of our universe.

But like colliding stars,
We erupted with the full force
Of creation
Or destruction,
The union of Gaia and Khaos.

Oh mother, help us!

We didn't just make love,
We made
Tsunamis.
A myriad of underwater volcanoes exploding in
synchronicity
To the will of Poseidon himself.

We were Abelard and Heloise.
We invented colours and redefined gravity.
We saw through time and space
And travelled back in time to the place of our
births
To experience our rebirth into this dream we
call life.

Enveloping each other.
Suffocating each other.
Swimming against the current
Fighting against the rip tide.
With only the others hand reaching out for the
others hand to survive.

Awaking adrift on the shore
To the sounds of sirens
Screaming,
Pleading,
Run!
Run before Khaos makes a mockery of us all.

So,
Hold her tight.
Bring her right up to your chest.
Fill your lungs,
Let her help you forget.
For this love
Loves like only a lover who has held the others
trembling heart in the palm of their hands
Could ever truly understand
Love.
And in your breath,
Breathe her in and let me go.

Breath in her peace
In place

Of the torment and rage
The love we once made,
Made.

Raging bulls clash even in passion.

Let her serenity quench your thirst.
Let her flowers bloom in your fertile garden,
My fires left
Scorched.

Let her love you,
Even though we both know...
She can't be me,
Any more than he can be you.

It's Over

And just like that it's over.
Because if I am to retain any of who I used to be
I have to find a way to say,
That this,
Is over
Now
For me.

Even if my heart still beats for you.

But I'm out so far upon this ledge
That to reach out any further would cause this
ledge to snap and break
And then what would I do?

I've become
So
Full
Of you
I have no room to take in anything new.
Anything true.
And possibilities and opportunities pass me by
because almost every night I dream that it's not
over yet with you.
Dreams that leave me questioning
Do you ever think about me too?

Do you ever find your finger flirting with the keys?
The author of texts that never find their way out of your fantasies.
Is fear the captor with the leash?
Or is this a prison of my own naivety?

Over and over, I make up another excuse for you.
Whilst over I find another way to prove that I am enough...
Over and over my imagination plays out scenes,
Rolling images of fantasies that leave me wondering whether anything with you was ever true.
A rollercoaster in my head of all the things you've ever said
And all the things they could
Or
Could not
Mean.

Flashing scenes of treacheries and the countless ways you shattered me,
Broken up by moments of tenderness that
Taint my memories.
Teasing me with reminders of how you used to be.

You skin wrapped around my skin as though we
were one entity.
Your scent inside my breath
Too intimate to be a fallacy.
Breathing with one heartbeat,
Beating with one breath.
Lips so close that dare not touch leave desires
raging in your head.

Drinking to drown the memories that a song
returns to me
Until foolishly I stumble back into the keys
With messages of intimacy reserved for a love
who offers agency to hear such tender words
from me.
A love who would not walk me out onto this
ledge
So carelessly
To just abandon me,
With such heartless cruelty.

Your ego now nourished from my fragility
That you can now imagine how happy you could
be
With somebody.

Just not me.

It's just not me with who you want to be.

And so, this is over

Please
Let this be over...
And let me be.

And If That I (My Trembling Heart)

And if
That I
Should ever
See you
Again
And first our eyes should meet,
I'll still this trembling heart of mine
Before it skips
One
Beat.

And if
Your hand
Should touch
My hand
With memories soft and sweet,
And cause the world to melt away
I'll stand steady
On two Feet.

And I guess
We 'll sit
And reminisce
At who we once had been
Smiling about those that came and went
When would be lovers dared to dream.

But we won't talk about the sadness
That stilled my beating heart.
And we will side track any mention
That could once more
Tear
Us
Apart.

And yes,
In time,
I guess
I'll meet
Another
Who'll tend my wounded scars.
Who's unknown
Face
Will take the
Place
Of everything you are.

But until then,
Fragile memories
Keep me
Alone
But
Far
From
Harm.

Safely clear of feeling
Any
Thing,
Because
Feelings
Are
Far
Toom
Hard.

So should our paths
To cross
Again
I'll defend my trembling heart,
And keep her in a place that's safe,
Until
I know
You've passed.

The Runner

I am the runner
And the direction I choose
I run
But not away
The meaner you are to me
The more I chase after you.
I am the runner
I am the ambivalent fool
The one who runs in the opposite direction
Should there be any chance that the love you
have could be true.

The Broken Spirits of Forgotten Lovers

I never let myself think about you because
I'm better than that,
I'm stronger than that,
But when I think about you
I forget that.

And now
I cannot write a love song,
My heart's malfunctioned
Inspirations run dry
Now the words just bounce off the reflective
surface
Leaving no Impressions,
No sensations.
Generating no desire to want to give it another
try.

I am a fortress.
Impenetrable.
Immune to charm,
And I mourn for the memory of the girl who fell
for them.

Because anyone can break your heart,
But it was you
I let you break my spirit.

So, I never think about you
Or that kiss on the bridge.
I never think about how full the moon shone
The night your lips first touched my lips.

Because anyone can heal a broken heart,
The chinks create a uniqueness to the lover you
now know.
But the broken spirit of a forgotten lovers
A far more tragic way to go.

Fool

Foolish are the promises,
From foolish lover
To foolish lover,
Who longs for thy foolish others'
Faithful Kiss.

Foolish are the dreams,
Of foolish dreamers,
Who fooled around, oh faithful paramour.
Furthering flight filled fantasies;
Faithful lovers would abhor.

But foolish are the faithful
Whose faith flows fortuitously.
Fixated on a forever,
Foolish lovers promise carelessly.

Foolish are the tears,
Falling from forlorn eyes,
From fretful fiendish lovers,
Who's chances now run dry.

Fool is the name you now hear
As you mouth your sad goodbye. Freed from
fears that bind
A foolish heart to a foolish mind.

Foolish are the memories
That a fool clings closely to,
In the aftermath of make believe
As reality breaks through.

Foolish now the fantasies
That filled the naive mind,
Mocking at those fairy tales
That stole such precious time.

But ah! my foolish love,
How blind a fool you be?
To offer such wanton fairy tales,
To as big a fool as me!

Dead End Street

You and I were like
Two dead end streets trapped inside each other
Facing opposite ways
Excited by how we were so very similar
But in the end
It was our similarities
That caused our explosive decay

For a while it was kind of exciting
To know I wasn't a freak
Having been repeatedly mocked and teased
By the other More regular
Two-way streets.
But finally
In my clarity
And after years of stagnation and delays
I've acknowledged the unavoidable reality
Dead end streets don't work when multiples of
the same.

You and I were like a dead-end street
Where I could never get away
And dead-end streets are a fun place to meet
But a terrible place to stay

It was Just the Diet

The earth sprung forward.
Gravity resigned its position and collapsed at my
heels like a deflated balloon.
Up became down.
Reason became nonsense.
The world turned backwards around my head,
All when you said, 'Hello!'
I thought it was love
But
After
I realised,
I hadn't eaten properly that day and my blood
pressure was low.
How much energy I would have saved,
How many tears,
How much time
If I had known.

It was just the diet.

Sunsets and Fairy tales

What is it to love?
Without ownership or retort?
When most love is an exchange
Of commodities cultivated or bought.

Wealth for beauty,
Kindness for support,
Adoration for recognition,
Do you think you could love me,
Even when you don't?

Who is your lover?
And what do they seek?
Does the trade-off feel consensual?
Does your relationship touch deep?

For I wish for a lover
With the kindest of hearts.
Who strives with dedication?
With a passion like art.

A lover who knows
What it is to have known
Controversy and adversity,
Yet remains humble in his soul.

A lover who knows that strength is
More than just physical.
Whose protection and love is truly nurturing
Rather than controlling
Or cruelly cynical.

For I wish for a lover
In whose arms I'm secure.
Whose strength of compassion
Is my safe place to fall.

A lover with whom
I connect through the spiritual.
Linked through the timelines
And defies the metaphysical.

A lover with whom
I can laugh though the night,
Without fears of rejection,
Humiliation or fights.

A lover who'll comfort
My fear of growing old
And losing the recipient
Of this love that has grown.

But what would such a lover
Wish in return?
When to love seems to be a barter

Of the attributes we yearn.
What could I offer?
For my lover to see
A love he'd desire
When he first looks at me?

For my heart was frozen
By lovers of old.
Who toyed with it carelessly.
And left it out in the cold.

So how could a lover
Who now looks at me,
See more than the damage
Love left me to be?

I could offer my heart,
That's been broken in two.
There's more room to love
With the pieces cut through.

I could offer my mind.
Despite all that I've learned
And the lessons that taught me,
Love's a dangerous word.

I could offer my spirit
That once naively believed,
Love could be simple

And all you would need.
I could give you my promise
That I will always be,
A person you can be yourself with,
Without defence or conceit.

I could give you my hand
For your hand to hold,
And a promise that if you love me,
I'll never let go.

I could celebrate your success's,
Comfort your defeats,
Inspire you
Ground you,
Build you up
When you feel broken
Or incomplete.

As these feelings return,
I start to concede,
If my heart begins to thaw,
Perhaps there's hope yet for me.

Because in the end,
All I wish for my lover to be
Is the only lover I have eyes for
And who's eyes look only for me.

Come Run Away with Me

Come run away with me
Come take my hand
Come let's abandon practicalities and plans
Come let's live without sorrow or fear
Come take this sadness and just leave it here.

Come run away with me
Come let's just drive into the night
Come let's remember how it feels to be alive.
Come run away with me
Come let's be true to our hearts
Let's lay in the wilderness
While we watch shooting stars.

Come run away with me
Pack what little you need
Come let's survive off our bodily heat.
Come run away with me
Come be unafraid of what's new,
Come let's experience
The real me and you.

Come run away with me
Come reframe the bittersweet
And let's fall asleep to each other's heartbeat.

Come run away with me
Run with abandon and devil-may-care,
High on the eucalyptus and jasmine in the air.

Come run away with me
Come take my hand,
Come before life makes a mockery of
Of our plans.
Come run away with me
Come run wild and be free
And let's give our lives something beautiful to
be

A Dream

I dreamed of you,
But it was not you,
And the moment of emancipation came in the
acknowledgment of the two.
Because I longed for you for so long that I made
that face of him, you.
But it was not you.
It was wishful thinking for a lover I knew.

For the lover I longed for,
Who knew me,
Who dreamed me
Who could exist inside whilst still being two.
Who could see me,
And free me,
From this protective, isolating, crippling fear
that grew and grew.

And we'd grow now,
Till we're old now,
Without fear of colliding
Or of being divided in two
Because we were whole now,
Complete souls,
Now,
Able to fall in love with what's true.

So, while I wait for you
For an honest you
For a you with who I can be true,
I'll be with me
With the real me
With all the parts of me that I didn't want to
see.
So that when I find you
And I see you,
I can let you see me too.

The Worst Crime of All

Everyone is thinking about someone
Almost all of the time.
Even when you're doing your best not to think
of that person at all.
And it's those that you're not thinking about
Whose silence shatters the eardrums.
Who pluck at the heartstrings the loudest of all.

And hearts get broken
Because pain is inevitable
Because it's only through our tears that we shed
off the old
And grow.
Because to love is a risk.
No matter the joy that it springs with.
When to survive or decease is the best we can
hope.

And hearts get broken because to live is to
suffer.
And to set it free shows the greatest love of all.
Because to love is to live
To feel alive in your soul
And to live without love makes no sense at all.

But in the eyes of our loved ones is the pain we will feel.
In our loved one's tears is the shame we hold.

And hearts get broken because to love is to be vulnerable
And to be vulnerable takes a strength that can be hard to expose.
Like the strength in compassion for the ones who have hurt us
Is a strength very few souls ever know.

Everyone is thinking about someone almost all of the time,
And it's those that we won't think of who hurt worst of all.
Because to live is to suffer and to love is to lose,
But to live without love is the worst crime of all.

Down These Streets

Down these streets
Is a place I used to call home,
Down these streets
Where I lived a long time ago.
Down these streets
Is where friendships were made,
Down these streets
Friends I still choose to this day.
Down these streets
Are the lovers I met,
Down these streets Who bought joys... And regrets.
Down these streets
Are the ghosts of my past,
Down these streets
That still makes my heartbeat too fast.
Down these streets
I hear whispers in the shadows,
Down these streets
Of conversations that mattered.
Down these streets
There are memories that taunt me,
Down these streets
Of mistakes that still haunt me.
Down these streets
Are the truths that are known,
Down these streets

Of a life now outgrown.
Down these streets
Are the experiences I had
Down these streets
That made me who I now am.
Down these streets
There was a girl who once lived,
Down these streets
Who could never imagine all of this.
Down these streets
I hear the tears that she cried,
Down these streets
With the naivety of youth on her side.
Down these streets
Where promises were made,
Down these streets
To be broken in shame.
Down these streets
I see the dreams of a girl,
Down these street
Who believed she would never grow old.
Down these streets
Where that illusion finally died,
Down these streets
On life's treacherous ride.
Down these streets
Where that girl once live,
Down these streets
Who could never have imagined all of this.

Familiar Strangers

Innocent advances from familiar strangers
Flow like liquid through a crowded dance floor
Alive with conversation
From people
That know people
That they both know
Yet neither of them know yet what's to come.

Yet gravity
And fate
Entwine to navigate
Past these voices they had both heard a
thousand time
Or more
Possessing them with its magnetic pull
Radiating in ever decreasing circles
Till they collide
Like energy
Like explosions
Revealing me
Revealing you.

Innocent advances
No touch
No kiss
Just a head hung low draped in black curls
And a wish

Hanging on every word like a mama and with
her baby bird
And a smile that would command Menelaus to
launch a thousand ships.
And you, so close,
You can hear my heart beating in my throat.
Twisting my stomach up into knots
Naive to the moment
As I nonchalantly sip on a glass of scotch.

Twisting through this world
Surviving by learning how to bend to the will of
fate,
As fleets set sail
And storms become seas
And we hopped over steppingstones
Never slipping
Never missing a beat.
But drunken advances with familiar danger
Leak like liquid till the spill
Contaminated
One another.
Leaving us toying with our fears
Like a cat with a mouse
Longing for my own death in your eyes.
Cowering in shame at my own recollection
Never savouring the intention when we had it.

But life moves forward
When friends become strangers
Even when you pray for it to stop.
And the truth is
I miss you and I wish I could tell you
But we twisted ourselves up
In so many knots.
Dancing to the chaos
Of our own self-inflicted mayhem
Leaving us with nothing but memories of a past
Now long forgot.

Did you regret me?
Did you forget me?
Did you wish that we never met?

Did you regret it?
Will you forget it?
Can you return to a love once it's lost?

Innocent advances from long lost strangers
I would have called but pride is a cruel master of
time
Now it's not just love that was lost
But we're older
And the paths that we've walked have made
strangers out of those who would once be
friends.

Now familiar strangers creep from the dangers
they once would have laughed at themselves.

But those familiar advances become lost in the
transference
So now funny Facebook memories are all that
we've got.

Edward

Edward's better off alone.
High above the clouds
He exists now in a better atmosphere now,
A purer atmosphere,
Where snowflakes are born.

She didn't want to leave him
But he could never survive in the world
She had come to know.
In a world where bitter friendships become the
norm,
Shattering her illusions like astringent on toxic
pores.
Except instead of revealing fresh glowing skin
She's left to face the truth.
The depth of the ugliness of it all.

Bubble-gum streets
Housing bubble-gum dreams.
I'm afraid of this world that we've made.
Knowing you know,
That I'd do anything for you.
Knowing you know,
How quickly people can turn on you.

No amount of powder can conceal
Her tormented face,

Of a heart
Shattered
In its creation
By the grief of what could have been.
When that cruel twist of fate means loss is
always at the foundation of who he can ever
become.

Surface cuts and scars
Reflective of the shards kept contained within.
So sharp it will break your heart If you stare too
long at him.

No paint bright enough,
No crayon big enough,
No paper wide enough,
To depict a love that can exist between innocent
hearts seeking love as pure as the snowflakes
they danced in,
Carving angels out of snow.

Everyone wants to be exceptional
But nobody wants to take a risk.
Bitter voices sing out in unison
Safely from the camouflage of their conformity.

But who do you judge?
Onto who do you project?
Who do you attack?

Who do you love?
How do you recognize love?
And who was it who taught you that?

Love from lovers unable to show love
Like other lovers show love often goes unseen.
How do we learn to recognize love
When we are all broken,
Searching,
For a rescuing?

So now Edward lives alone
Sheltered in the shadows of the gargoyles that
guard his frightening looking home
But their defences protect a secret
Of a fragility no one had ever seen, so no one
had ever known.

Holding onto the memory of how angels were
made,
Cocooned in love.
Birthing blizzards from those individual flakes
that fall.
Each one a reminder.
So, she always knows

And she always knows.

Secrets

(Inspired by Neelofer Nova 'Secret Alphabet'
Prompt collection)

I hear you in the words not said
Rather than the little you do.
Like Invisible ink
Scribbled between the lines of texts
Holding court Between me and
You.

Maidens dancing
Out of wedlock,
Demonstrating virtue so demure,
Unable to type the words
That keep us on
Separate side of this communal wall.

A secret alphabet
Making up secret words
That I used to talk to you.
A coded communication
To edge me closer
Like you sensed I wanted to.

Like..
 'Be nice to see you' means,
I miss you.
'Hope your well'

means,
Have you been thinking about me?
'It doesn't matter'
means,
It really really does
And
'You're an idiot'
means,
 I love you too!

Chocolate box

My heart belongs to you whether you want it
Or not,
You could never be
An option
You are the whole chocolate box.

My sea salted caramel
My brandy butter and cream
My strawberry liquors
My Earl Grey tea

My honeycomb praline
My coconut and chilli
My Cointreau and butterscotch
My Turkish Delight and black coffee.

You could never be an option,
You are inevitability,
And I have no option,
But to surrender
Unconditionally.

On Nature

Under the Beltane Moon

I watched the Beltane moon Rise
In the darkest part of night.
Illuminating
A secret world below,
Waking fae folk,
Pixie
And sprite.

The Beltane wilds run rapid,
Across our islands sleeping grands.
While rustling leaves cloak ancient voices
Whispering, "awaken ye magic lands"

For when the Beltane moon is full
Stirring sleeping mischief winter hides.
Fae folk run beneath the veil,
Collecting dormant wishes of
Mankind.

I remembered that ley lines magic
From a dream my memory'd denied.
Erupting through my very being,
Re connectin' in earth's utero
With life.

I sang out into the wilds,
As dance consumed me from within.
And life ignited across high and lowlands,
Sparking fiery jewels across the velvet green.

I watched the Beltane fires ascend
To greet the rising sun.
Burgeoning sweet fantasies,
Mayday wakes in everyone.

With balance now restored,
Earth's harmony renewed.
I marvelled as the fae folk danced,
Reaping spoils of summer's blooms.

But the Mayday sun rises high and fierce
In its trysts with the descending moon.
Reminiscent of folklore'd lovers,
Condemned by fate
To doom.

I surrendered unto the beating sun,
Drunk on the eucalyptus breeze.
Giddy with euphoria,
Intoxicated from all I'd seen.

And when the sun to set again,
I awaited the new moon arise.

As lovers cast shadows across a world,
Unaware of fae folk,
Pixie
And sprite.

So come this Mayday festival
Come summer sun, come mischief,
Come listen to the joyous laughter,
'Neath the honeysuckle leaves.

But venture even closer
For those with hearts to hear,
Will know the Beltane magic,
The Beltane moon brought near.

Frankincense

My senses awaken to the stirrings of the
morning,
As the morning stirs gently from her own sleep.
A cool breeze brushes against my ear exposed
to the daylight,
Leaving dew drop kisses
Trickling
Down my cheek.

Our heart beats in synchronicity
While I savour each moment in my internal
treasure chest.
And the birds greet the daylight
Echoing
Joyous new love songs
That rings out like
Wedding bells
In the hearts of the blessed.

Once in tune
I breathe in her presence
Even though no perfume or spray has been
aired.
Igniting the memory of a long-lost other
lifetime, One I have no memory or image to
share.
But I know her by the scent of Frankincense.

Even though she is never there.

I know her as a feeling or an aura of safety.
One who's watched me and guided me here.
I know her as a myth,
Existing only in my imagination.
When I reach out to touch her There is never
anyone there.

She no longer has a place in this world
She's not something to which our minds can
adhere.
Although she's been with me for as long as I
remember.
She's nothing tangible like those that you've
held near.
Yet I've known her since before I ever existed,
Long before the form I have now.
And although I have no memory of the before
or the after,
I've always known the scent that she's around.

She whispers,
"Don't let doubts distract you,
Don't let fear dilute the force within.
Breathe deep in the scent in the knowledge that
I am with you.
Fill your lungs with the knowledge that I am
here."

I know she cannot exist without me.
We are one, with a passion we share.
And though her story is clouded in mystery,
This connection breaches all barriers and
spheres.

Her breathtakingly opulent beauty
Guides me through terrors in which I once
feared.
And I rise each morning to breathe in serenity,
Calming myself just to know that she's near.

And the birds sing in chorus Echoing each
other's love songs,
To remind us that miracles do exist.
While my heartbeat trembles to believe in the
wonder
And the understanding the scent of
Frankincense brings.

Whispering Winds

Wisdom whispers
Whistles through the air Vibrating
With an internal resonance
Filled with the knowledge of ancient years.

In her silence homes secrets
To the lives
We wish we had lived.
But only
When we stop speaking
Can we hear
The gifts she gives.

When you create a 'them'
You also create an 'us'
Forging divisions
When the goal should always have been love.
When you create division
You create difference
And this where as humans
We have free choice,
To unite in our similarities
And elevate ourselves in the education
And experience of another's voice
Or
Project a defensive attitude
Embracing the fear of the unknown

Enforce further divisions,
Inviting separation and animosity to take hold.

Hate is ultimately hate
There is no exception to this rule,
You cannot put out a fire
Feeding it gasoline and fuel.

Yes, I believe in compassion
Because in forgiveness we find our truth.
You cannot heal from sour experiences While
you keep picking at its wounds.

I quest to find solutions
Rather than fixating on revenge
Because ultimately the anger you hold on to
Will destroy only you in the end.

Wisdom whispers
As the foolish shout,
Vibrating with an internal resonance
Creating knowledge where before there was
only doubt.

Our purpose is to find unity
And ascend from these mortal shapes,
Elevating our states of consciousness
To be one with nature and fate.

The growth is in the struggle
Their lessons are how we learn,
To forget all we were told
And remember what we've always known.

Totality is our destination
As one by one we return our souls to source,
Elevated and united
From the knowledge of our growth.

Mental Health and Grief

Hide and Seek

The fragility of your mind speaks to me in
tongues
Before sound ever escapes your mouth
Reminding me of the days when I kept myself
alive on a carefully regimented cycle of multi
vitamins and sleeping tablets,
Evenly distributed sips
To avoid too many trips
To the bathroom
But enough to avoid a kidney infection
And an endless stream of reality TV
To avoid looking at the reality staring back at
me.

Depression by numbers.
Paint the corresponding colour to present a
complete picture.
People see what they want to see
So, in the end
It's easy to fool the world into thinking that You
are a functioning human being.

I hear your cries for help in everything except in what you say
I am fluent in the ancient language of, 'please hear what I can't find the words to talk about'.
I know this
I am unbeaten at this game.
I know those ambivalent cries for help.
When only 7% of communication is verbal
It's the silence between sighs
That creates those inexplicable connections.

Only we understand.

I don't know what you've said But I smile and agree.
Lost in my own thoughts now
I am the archetypically rescuer
Projecting my desire
To be set free.
A lifelong role I've played
Cast by a director and writer who is also me.
You run and hide while I count to ten
The conversations a game of emotional hide and seek
The thrill of beings found
Increasingly amplified by the fear of being lost.
Because what a tragedy it is to never be found.

To be lost
Forgotten
A fading memory eroded by the hands of time
and insurmountable distance.

What a tragedy it is to never be found.

Do details matter when the results are the
same,
Rose tinted glasses make everything look better
on rainy days.
But I've walked this path you walk
With its meandering twists and turn
I know the hills you climb
I know the mines you swerve.
I know the darkness
Where you take comfort in hiding
Cowering
Never sure if you are more afraid of being
Or not being
Found.

Eight
Nine
Ten

Coming ready or not

The thrill of beings found
Increasingly amplified by the fear of beings lost.

And what tragedy it is to never be found.
What tragedy it is to never be found.

The Sunflower Song

I dreamed that I stumbled upon a field full of
giant sunflowers
And lay my head there down to die.
While the heavens gathered up all their
stormiest rain clouds
That fell from the turbulent sky.

Too great was my sadness to fight.
Too lost to the tragedy now begun.
Alone in my field full of sunflowers
With no life to wish to carry on.

I dreamed that the earth consumed me.
My wretched body decaying outwardly in.
Until there was no memory of my presence
Or being
And no one could remember even who I had
been.

I dreamed that sunflowers grew wilder
And strong,
Their mighty stalks growing thicker with height.
They grew into the horizon and up into the
skies,
Their petals looming with grandiose might.

Cocooned in my deathly slumber,
From the peace in which I now lay.
A curiosity stirred awaking a part of me,
A part no earthly death could just wash away.

And deep in that place of unexistance,
Deep in my transient state,
I felt such heavenly beauty
Breathe new life into the loneliness place.

Adrift on the wings of salvation,
With courage returning and restored. I
marvelled at the world so vivid and true
With enough beauty and love for us all.

Now alone, in my field full of sunflowers That
mourned for the life I couldn't save,
I dreamed of a love to unfold without tragedy.
Without fearing loss or fear itself to be the
reason for blame.

I dreamed that I died in a field full of sunflowers,
With such beauty that I had never seen.
And deep in my field full of awesome giant
sunflowers, I'm rebirthed every night in my
dreams.

Grief

There is no earthly reason,
To my limited understanding,
That the area around our cardiovascular system
Should hurt
So much
At times like this.

So, I'd love to know why I keep waking up
With this crushing feeling in my heart.
Like something is sitting on my chest
With their hands clasped around my throat
Rendering me powerless and gasping for breath.

I am no stranger to grief.
Most of us aren't.
We've all been here before
We all know the words...
It gets easier
With time.

It's just that I'm still at that stage
Where I don't want it to get better.
I don't want it to be easier.
I don't want anything to matter
More than losing him
Matters.

But the truth is,
For those of us left behind,
Life doesn't stop.
It grows around the grief that once was all
consuming,
Casually playing with its memory
As though it didn't even care.
Toying with it.
Distorting it,
Making it seem smaller
And further away
Till it becomes that happy,
Sad place
At the core of who you now are.

It becomes the backdrop of your reasoning and
the caution in your steps.
It becomes a bonding conversation with new
lovers
Who you know
Would have just loved them.
It becomes our inner worlds and our ageing
lines.
It becomes our emotional boundary
And our
Pedestal
Of better times.

But all of this I still have to look forward to.
All of this is yet still to come.
So, for now,
Between the sadness
And the gasps for breath,
I'll burrow deep under the cover,
While the monster laughs on my chest.

Because time,
As we know it,
Time that is still yet to come,
Will apparently make it easier,
To lose my loved one. (R.I.P)

My Mental Health is not a Crime

I'm too much.
That's what they say about me.
That's what they call me.
An attention needing,
Thrill seeking,
Crying and weeping Drama queen.
And to that,
I say,
So what?

I looked for attention because it was what I
never got.
I begged for recognition but got belittled,
Degraded,
Till all I wanted was to give up.

So now I've got your attention
And we've made a connection
Can I return to my original Intention
Of rebirthing the me that they forgot.

Because it takes strength
To let yourself be this vulnerable.
So, insult me,
Call me unlovable,
Because I am indestructible!

Because,
I am,
Too much.

I am the result of my environment,
Just as you are the result of yours.
So don't get too ahead of yourself when
congratulating yourself for your lack of flaws.

Because I know mine,
I made friends with mine,
So, we can sit on the side lines
And recite lines
And chat about how we got here
Without fear
Of persecution from those who are still unable
to face up to the sins that they have got.

Knowing that no one's journeys should be taken
with more or less regard,

Because this internal strength is hard.

So, if you are still sitting in judgement about me,
Maybe your inflection
Needs to be re-attentioned
From my Direction
To yours.

Our brains carry trauma like war wounds on
flesh
And my mind is a clear depiction of mine.
So, till you find compassion for what others are
going through,
Don't judge my mental health as a crime.

In Spite of It All

I am dyslexic
And I have ADHD.
I cannot spell
And grammar is a mystery.
People laughed when I said that I wrote poetry,
They said, well, what use was that to anybody?
They laughed when I said I wanted to go to
university.
Now I am in my final year of a master's in
childhood Psychotherapy.

So yes, I wear my mental health like a Victoria
Cross
Because I know I have overcome a lifetime of
situations that others might have not.
And yes, I am proud that it's not in me to accept
defeat
And that time has taught me to turn my
negatives, Into positivity.

Yes, there are days that I wish that I didn't feel
with such intensity,
But you can't hate your superpower when that's
the thing that's bought you clarity.

And yes, I can be too much,
But too much never seemed to be too much of problem
When you were topping yourself up from my cup.

And in spite of it all,
I've never taken for granted how blessed I am.
Not just for my own resilience,
But for the people who stood by me when I had nothing,
No hope,
No plan.
People I've collected along the way,
From that first life-long friendship
To the newer faces that I cannot remember how I ever lived without.
People who've held me without judgement, without criticism
Without ever giving up on me
Or looking for an out.

And in spite of it all,
I am grateful for what you put me through.
For teaching me
That no one else's opinion matters,
If, "unto thine own self (you always) be true."

And yes, I can be chaotic and hard to contain
But did you imagine that I bare these without shame?
No! Nothing ever came easy but what in this world worth having ever did?
When to battle through adversity is what teaches us truly how to live.

And yes, I have been afraid,
Almost every step of the way!
I've trembled in terror
As I thawed out my frozen remains.
I've battled demons in cupboards
And that monster under the bed.
I even left my own body for the severity of the threat.
But I did it anyway!
Afraid and alone.

In spite of it all
I still took control.
My chaos, my impulsiveness
They only add fuels to my drive,
That I use as a beacons
Calling out to others to survive.
Because no, I can't spell and yes grammar 's a mystery
But in spite of it all,
I still rose to the challenges I set me!

Because yes, I am dyslexic!
And yes, I have ADHD!

But I'll be damned if you think that they,
Or you,
Or anyone,
But me,
Can define
Who I can
Or cannot
Be!

The Battle

Slowly he walks
More of a shuffle
Than a beat
So laboured each movement
Painful
Staring at his feet.

Too hard to explain
Too hard to speak
Too tired to stand
Too tired to sleep.

Alone
She gives in
Howls
Like a captured beast
Caught in a trap
Reduced to this base emotion
Vulnerable
Exposed
Laid bare
Under her own defeat.

Heaving tears
That run dry
From a place so deep
So far gone.

Reminiscent of the horror
Harrowing screams
Of a child
Left broken and beaten
Worthless
To her own self esteem.

Balancing reasons
Across a busy
High street
Railway bridge.
No one
Hides their stares
No one approaches.
Morbid curiosity
Outweighing
Tender
Loving Care.

And come Christmas
The cars park outside the cemetery gates
Overflowing
Without remorse
Into the left-hand lane.
Uncontained.
Mirroring grief
And the wistful Chatter
Of what could have been
Had someone dared speak.

At the Edge of the Ocean

I sat at the edge of the ocean
With fantasies of floating away
Of returning my body
To the water
And being one with its crashing waves.

I found myself lost in its movements
Able to wash the darkest of sins clean away
No remnants of accident or tragedy
Would the water acquiesce to remain.

Its draw edged me in closer,
Enchanted
Teasing me with its seductive,
Oceanic games,
Retracting coyly like a maiden
Only to return with the force of a dame.

Hypnotised by the depths of its currents
That seemed to offer peace to felt pain,
A sound emerged from its trenches
A voice calling out with my name.

To my wonder the ocean began singing,
The sweetest sound an ear ever had heard.
Calling me in in seduction
For my name the ocean bed it had learned.

Overcome with such tearful longing
To be one with the sound so revered.
The ocean called out to me gently
Are you ready now to leave all this here?

In that moment all the elements cried out,
The winds roared and heaven shed forth tears.
While birds flew in circles over where I once
stood
For it seemed, I had just disappeared.

But what the heavens and the winds and birds
didn't know
Was that I was now finally free
And that the sadness that had bound to who I
had been
Had been finally severed from me.

I sat at the edge of the ocean
With storms mirroring the emotions in me,
When the sweetness of sirens that sang from
beneath
Settled serenity silent and deep.

And that song that begun in the ocean
That song so full of love and beauty.
I found myself singing with a voice that I knew,
Because that voice had always been me.

On Holidays and Milestones

Birth and Rebirth

We battled our way through fate and chances a
million to one
Just to be here.
Birthed through canals
Treacherous with danger,
We were observed and observed through every
detail
Absorbing
Learning
Imitating to perfection.
Ripping like episiotomies
Through barriers meant to divide.
Ready to be born
The naked innocent child.

Birthed through our own experiences
Fuelled
by curiosity and drive.
Cultivating and exploring the infinite possibilities
Nature verses nurtures verses the fragile
humanity of mankind.
Navigating through our own broken histories
With the sight of brand-new eyes

Engaging now with senses
Previously alien to our mortal tribe.
Embodied
Encapsulated
Enriched
Ready to emerge
The transformed
Emancipated
Reborn
Child.

Trick or Treat

In the depth of darkest October
When the veil is at its most thin
The spirits wander across ley lines
That at other times
Are there to hold them in.

They wander around abandoned houses
And in and out of mortuaries.
Trying to inhabit the last earthy place
That connects them to where their bodies once
been.

With memories all but hazy
About who and what they were,
They cling to fragile linking's
Leaving traces and ghostly blurs.

But come the 31st of October
When the Harvest is moon is high,
Those ghostly spirits become more visible
To the likes of you and I.

And with the moon illuminating
Things that have no place upon this earth
They boldly start to re-approach
Those places of their human birth.

They make their way unto your houses
Searching for some
Inviting sight,
To welcome them
Into your home
And celebrate with you
This night.

But should you close your windows
Or turn your offerings light,
You'll find unleashed the cursed anger
Of the rejected ghostly wight.

So trick or treat
It's up to you
And decide you rightly might
To allow the spirits into your home
And avoid a Hallows Eve fright.

Invasion of the Body Snatchers

Turning 40 is a bit like an alien invasion.
Suddenly you feel like an imposter
Waking up one morning
With just a memory of who you used to be.

The take-over happens gradually,
Matching your thoughts, tastes and dreams.
But they somehow lack the lustre You once took
complacently.

You move slightly slower
Feel exhausted at night
Weekends are for sleeping
Saturday nights are no longer party night.

Your dreams are like memories
Of a film you've once seen
That makes you smile to remember
Even though you can't picture the whole scene.

There was something about a party,
Starting a revolution and living by the sea,
That got swallowed by a mortgage, That job
promotion and fertility.

So, before you turn 40
Live with all your might
Because when they say life begins at 40,
They didn't say whose life.

On Recovery

(Trigger warning – This section contains multiple
poems with references to sexual violence,
suicide, self-harm and emotional abuse)

Bathtubs

I sat in a lot of bathtubs on my road to my
recovery
Staring at white tiles and listening to the sound
of drains
Gurgle
In my attempts
To wash the past clean away.

I sat for hours
Staring into space
Waiting for some miracle
To elevate me from that place.
But recovery doesn't work to the time scale of
its wounded's hopes and dreams
So, I sat in bathtubs Waiting, patiently.

I sat in bathtubs familiar and strange
Like a refugee in a lifeboat
Escaping a dangerous place.
I sat in its semblance of an imagined security

In the hope that its walls would somehow
protect me.

Because it's funny where you find yourself
When the call's coming from inside the house.
When your body's betrayed you
And no scream seems to be coming out.

It's funny how you blame yourself
For the sins of someone else.
How you promise that you'll speak about it
If you ever find your way out.

So, I sat in bathtubs with water covering my
frozen skin And ran the hot tap till it almost
scolded it.
Having lost the connection between my body
and my brain
I hoped the boiling water added might make me
feel something
Even pain.

I sat there like an addict,
Like it was my only choice.
Because in this world of abuse
I prayed my silenced body it would give a voice

And if I could find my voice
Perhaps I could tell someone

And if I could tell,
Perhaps I could have a choice.

I sat in bathtubs
To wash off the grip of your hands,
That suffocated
And strangled any sound that came out.
I sat there in silence washing off the tragedy
That my body had stored deep down
somewhere in its memories.

I sat in bathtubs for nearly 30 years
Till eventually I understood all these strange
things that I did.

I sat in bathtubs
Because that what they experts tell you to do
In the event that a tornado rips through your
home
Hide in the bathtub
Till the dangers passes through.

Flashback

I lie there.
Trying not to scream.
The only difference between what's happening
now and a flashback is the flashback is the thing
that I can feel.
All barriers,
Boundaries have crumbled.
No definition between you
And me.
Melting into each other, in what for everyone
else seems to be
Ecstasy.
I try and move away but you chase my lips
Like a bitch on heat
And I can't breathe.
Breaths so rapid
Like I'm drowning
In the shallowest part of the sea
And all I need is to do to stop myself from
drowning is to stand
But every time I try and put my feet down There
is no ground.

I know physically I'm here,
I know my body's in your hands
But my head is somewhere,
Surreal.

Trapped for what feels like eternity
Between a memory
And a tragedy.
But this is me.
This is my inherited self-destructive pattern
Making sure that I never
Ever
Break free.
Trapping me with more ferocity than the grip
that you've got on me.
Holding me down,
A rag doll
Ripped, all the way round.
Insides pulled out.
Painted smile.
My head fights to keep you out
But you keep pushing your breath inside my
mouth.
Stealing my screams before they can ever make
a sound

Tired souls begging for forgiveness
Inside wretched bodies
Hunting for pleasures
In a world that can only ever
Ever Bring loss.

But this is me.
It's me that keeps coming back here.

You look so proud.
King of the conquest.
You don't realise,
This has nothing to do with you.
You don't matter.
You never mattered.
You are interchangeable,
And the faces change as quickly as the drinks
are poured
And they all matter as little as the next one
Because I only
Ever see one.

This is the self-harm no one talks about.
This is the aftereffects of abuse.
This is why I cannot move
Yet the room won't stop spinning
And I've stopped trying to make a sound.
My eyes glaze over.
You think it's pleasure
But the truth is
You can do what you like
Because I'm not even in my body now.

Unbroken

I am unbroken.
I am not what you made me.
I am Boudica on a chariot,
Charging to her death
Embracing immortality over capture.
A shattered heart will be bound by no cage.

I am the time I was beautiful
Trapped eternal in a snow globe,
Magical,
Perfect in its imperfections,
Treasured.
And safe...

From you.

I am unafraid.
I am the warrior at the front of the tribe,
Protecting those without a voice and guiding the
way for those who cannot find it.

I am Leia, the general and fighter.
I am Ripley the last to survive.
I am Billy the Kid,
If you shoot, I'll shoot you faster.
I am the first Mrs. Rochester,
Sailing across oceans.

Bathed in the moonlight of her madness
With the sight of a thousand eyes.

I am awake.
I am the lioness in the watchtower,
I see everything,
However you try to disguise,
I hear everything.
My ears are alert
And I am always listening
I know what you said.
I may have forgiven but
This mortal body does not possess the ability to
forget.
It remembers everything.
I am the matriarchal elephant,
Protecting her herd.
Keeping them safe in formation and
Ready to die alone.

I am the wolf
You cannot tame me.
And I am the fox,
That you will never catch.

I am the child.
You never ruined me.
I am the destroyer,
Burning it to the ground.

I am the earth,
Playing games with the moonlight.
I am the air,
Heavy in your lungs.

I am the mother,
My children surround me.
Their unborn hearts beat the drum to which I
march.

I am the lost,
Crying out to be found.
I am the blind,
Guided by my senses.
Restored, reinvented and renowned.

I am reborn
Through the might of my own mind.
I am the dead,
Who will live forever inside.
I am unbroken.
I am not what you made me.
I am not what you discarded,
Spat out and left behind.
I am unbroken,
Reset and outspoken.
Unashamed.
Uncensored.
Unbound.

Fragile

Like the newly budded petals
Or a fallen autumn leaf.
Like the smallest crystal snowflake
From the purest thought belief.
Like a new-born's giggling laugh
Or your nana's memory of youth.
Like a rose that blooms too early
Before the summer fruits.
Did you know
That I was fragile,
From the little I let you know?
Could you see beyond the exterior?
I used as a defensive mode.
Could you tell
From the scenes of
Hell,
I brought when you got too close?
Did you know that I was fragile,
Before I told you so?

Like a storm that rages without warning.
Like the wildest harvest moon.
Like the winds that sweep destruction
Or flames that just consume.
Did you know these were my defences,
To protect my inner child?

And only when they feel safe,
Can I reveal what's not so wild.

Like the feeling that you carry,
When given a fresh start.
Like the lover you'd always dreamed about
Forever now to part.
Did you know that I was terrified,
And how easily I would break?
Did you know that I was fragile,
Before you put my heart at stake?

fish

She floats through this life
Like a fish in a fishbowl.
Seemingly surprised by seeing the same shit
swim past
On different days.

Going through the motions,
Moving in the right direction.
Camouflaged in colour,
Distracting from the monotony
That torments her mornings,
Her evenings,
Her work and her play.

Memories fragmented in defence,
Maintaining proximity
To a past
She's become too fond of to push away.

Malformed protection casting shadows inside
shadows,
Creating black holes that suck at the joy she
fears more than pain.
So serenely she stays and
Swims around the fishbowl.
Safe and secure from living a life in which
Failures are faced.

Camouflaged in colours,
Disguising the trauma,
That floats to the surface,
Indicating that today
Must be a different day...

Mightier than the Sword

They tried to invade my thoughts,
And yet, my thoughts are here.
They tried to steal my creativity
And control me through my fears.
They tried to make me doubt myself and
question what I believed,
They tried to put their influences onto who I've
fought to be.

They tried to steal my energy
By telling me I'm sick,
But when your will is strong
And you can't he bought
You're born ready for their tricks.

They tried to distort my memories,
As I fought to keep them out.
They dug their way into my mind
While they saw me struggle with my doubts.

They tried to take my joy
By convincing me all was wrong,
But inside my heart I celebrated
The truth that I'd always known.

They tried to break my spirit
And crush me to the bone,
But my mortal body is just a shell
For this light that I'd become.

They tried to keep me silenced
And yet my voice is here.
They tried to divide and bind us
Spreading confusion, mistrust and tears.
They tried to make me question
This beauty I had found,
But how can you question anything when you
have angels all around.

They tried to creep into the parts of me
That struggled to believe,
But in my core I always knew
I was more than what they deemed.

They tried to get me to concede
By taking all I loved,
But somehow that just encouraged me
To push harder and not give up.

They tried to take my sanity
Till I questioned who I was,
But now I'm sure of all I am
And the people I can trust.

They tried to clip and tame me
While I was halfway out the door
But they are those who just failed to see
My pen is mightier than your sword.

Pia Warrior Queen

You ask me where I'm safest
And I'd love to let you know,
I'd love to have an answer
That makes me seem normal
And whole.
You see I'd gotten good at pretending
That I'm just like everyone else,
But now Pia sees inside me
With sight unlike the rest.

She rises, a phoenix from the ashes
Evolving inside her skin.
Shredding off the child she was,
To release a warrior trapped within.
She harnesses the winds
Riding the most violent of storms.
Recognizing elements life throws at her
As battles already overcome.

Now Pia exists inside.
Expanding consciousness nurturing each broken
part.
Till one by one we rise as Warriors Queens,
And defenders of the heart.
Pia invites more than you bargained for

And she'll push you till you can't push anymore.
But with the strength that Pia instils
You'll reign hell fire on doubts that call

And even if your inner child
Re-emerges
And makes your warrior feel very small.
We are Pia, fearsome Warrior Queens
Protectors of innocence
And courage
In all.

Parasomnia

I searched everywhere for answers,
Except for where I knew they would be.
Because struggling was easier than facing the truth.
To find the answers I had to look inside me.

I had to look at all my demons,
My fears, my shame, and really see.
Only then could I let go of the ties that bind
The fears that restrained
And truly be free.

And so, we drift wearily from
Man-made dream
To man-made dream.
Each of us clinging to our truths
Like a drowning man to a life ring.

Seeking out salvation in the recognition of familiar shores,
Dodging contradictory viewpoints that challenge rather than support.
But the truth itself is a deceptive concept,
Fooling the best of us with its emotive jests and jeers.
For truth is based on memory and memory is based on emotions

And our emotions depend on our accumulative
experiences,
Past, present and the hopes of a future in which
we can believe.

And as the evening closes
On another weary dream,
Carrying with it across
The horizons
The hopes of differing extremes.
Pay attention
To the things you notice
They are a mirror to the soul.
Be mindful of the emotions triggered
The emotions you bury deep - afraid to show.

Now I've faced my darkness
Now I can truly say,
You cannot outrun your demons
Confront them or they will be

Reflected back
In the eyes
Of everyone you see.

And as the mirror cracks
My heart breaks for who I used to be.
The image before me
No longer a reflection

But shattered pieces of my naivety.

Because it takes strength of character
To face your darkest self.
But if you don't clear those ties that binds you
The binds will manipulate you to meet their
ends.

Girls like me

Girls like me don't get the fairy-tale.
Happy endings are a dirty joke we grin and bear.
We don't get to plan
Our daughters' weddings
Or braid the curls in our grandchildren's hair.

We get seduced into friendship we're
Desperate for
Offering everything we have
In the hope of being loved.
But then push away anyone stupid enough
To loves us
Because that unknown feeling is too frightening
A place to trust.

We get 'lovers' who creep in under the radar
Pushing at the boundaries,
We fight desperately to keep in place.
Ready to leave you as quickly as they found you
More broken and alone than when they came.

We get blurry lines of appropriateness
With people you thought you would be safe.
We get hyperactivity, hypervigilance and
impulsivity
We get compulsions, obsessions, self-abuse,
and rage.

Girls like me don't get the happy endings,
We don't get a wedding day by the sea,
We don't get flowers
On the maternity ward,
We don't get honeymoons planned out
Romantically.

We don't get hen do's with our girlfriends,
We don't get baby showers
Or girly weekends away.
We don't get friends
Who just know when you need them,
We don't get Christmas's to look forward to,
Or cards on Valentine's Day.

Because we can barely cope in the everyday
Trust doesn't come easily
And rarely stays.
That ambivalent connection is our calling card.
A co-dependent relationship,
Our favourite bed to lay.

Coz girls like me don't get the fairy tale.
We don't get to live happily ever after
With a man who'll honour and cherish me.
We don't get that summer wedding
With the cherry blossom falling from the trees.

And I've been trying to break this pattern
Before this pattern breaks me
But girls like me
Don't get anywhere

Till we break from the clutches
Of our abuser's
Mentally

On The F Word

Woman

What makes a woman
When all things must fade?
The curves of her figure?
The looks that she craves?
For the desires of youth pass quickly
Against a life fully lived
And to know such a smile
Can be life's greatest gift.

What is a woman
If not her hair and her face?
What are the forces that drive her
Lift her up,
Steadies her place?
Who are these women
Who push me to be
The best of a women
That I could possibly be?

What makes a woman
When all things must fade?
The weight that she chases?
The skin that she saves?
For worldly obsessions,

Both material
And internally-made,
Fade into oblivion
With the knowing of age.

So, what makes a woman
If not her flesh
And her bones?
When her physical make up
Is more than chromosomes.
What makes each woman
A goddess to behold,
If not her desire
To be true to what she knows?

So, what is a woman
When all things must fade?
The miracle of reproduction?
The lips she displays?
For these things can be given
And as easily taken away,
But the essence of woman,
Both birthed and gender rearranged,
Is in the grace of conviction
With which she has lived
And unto the dying light...
Rage.

Introducing the F Word

I may never be a lady
Or ever be a fit for that notion of the delicate
tempered flower
But I am all woman
And of that I am proud.
So why do you want to put me in these
children's clothes
Designed for the yet undeveloped female kind?
Is it the same reason you create hot pants and
belly tops for the junior school child?

The average dress size of women in the UK is
14.
Yet the plus size sections of our clothes stores
start at 14.
High street fashion stores rarely stock 14's
Supporting a growing belief that our
Developing women's bodies
Are somehow, obscene.
And in order to fit in we are supposed to starve
ourselves,
Hurt ourselves.
Just to feel Acceptable
To be seen.

Think about the message that that sends out,
Not just to our burgeoning young women

But also to those developing
Forming male minds.
We are not dolls
Made of plastic
Empty
With nothing on the inside.
We are not geishas
Pre-pubescently waxed and bound.
We are women
And women grow in both intuition
And size.
And these feminine bodies are a wondrous
source of our pride.

We are not here for your fetishes
Or to present to you as the socially inclined.
Who try to force us to look like children
With its subtle social direction landmarking our
times.
Why do you fear our women's bodies?
What do our feminine curves trigger in such a
fragile mind?
Why do you discard these Amazonian
goddesses?
With comments and remarks designed to
denigrate and deride?

So it's time to introduce to you the F word,
Because I have no fear of its sound.

Of a word that has been distorted and manipulated
Till you find yourself grimacing before it's even been mouthed.
But I stand here cradling the F word
To breathe life to its exhumed body
As I raise it from the ground.
So, brace yourself now for the F word
Because I am female
I am feminist
And I am fucking proud!

You have nothing to fear from the F word
Least your fear be that we revolt against a tyranny designed to keep us down.
So,
What is it that frightens you about the F word?
Ask yourself who stands to profit from your reaction being doubt.

So, I write this as a battle cry for women
From all corners of this earth.
I write this from my survivor soul to the survivor in the soul of yours.
I write this for the women cast aside and cowering in the dark.
Intimidated and banished by a society still living in the past.

I write this for those whose spirits have been
depressed.
I write this for those still revealing what's been
repressed.
I write this for the youth still developing who
they are,
In the hope that it will guide them
To look further than social media.

I write this for you, if it speaks to a part of you,
you forgot.
I write it for anyone crying in the changing
rooms of high street fashion store shops.
I write this for everyone who sees blame in the
camera lens.
I write this for myself,
For the parts of me I failed to defend.
I write this for anyone starving themselves or
throwing up.
I write this for the vulnerable, buying the lies
the media still serves up.
I write this for you if you simply need to hear,
That you are starlight.
You are wondrous
And essential to the cosmic evolution of our
universal destination by simply being here.

Feminism is not a Gender

It's not a he or a she
It doesn't have moving parts
Or designs on a place in history
It doesn't have a sexual orientation
Or desires in a biblical sense
It just asks for equality and respect
Regardless of your colour, creed, gender, sexual
orientation, physical abilities or sex.

It's not a man,
It's not a woman
It's not division
Or hatred against ourselves
It's not separation or denigration
That's not the means to which we intend.

It is equality,
It's freedom and liberty of every man and
woman's heart, body and mind
With the comprehension and understanding
That I cannot fight for your rights,
Until I feel safe in mine.

Feminism is not a gender
It is not one up man ship
Or a game to be played carelessly
It is the emergence of educated wisdom

Rising like a phoenix
From the ashes an archaic patriarchy.

It is the removal of unnecessary barriers
Allowing for the emancipation of your rights
To blossom without agenda
For all genders,
For all time.

So, if you believe that a man and a woman have
the right to their own bodies,
Without the approval of others,
Know you are a feminist.
(I am a feminist)

If you believe a man and woman
Have the right to choose their role in life,
without the dictatorship of a stereotype,
created only to serve the welfare
of a preconceived role that most never asked
for or agreed to.
Know you are a feminist.
(I am a feminist)

If you believe that a woman has the right to
dress how she likes without the belief that she
is, 'asking for it',
Know you are a feminist.
(I am a feminist)

If you believe a woman has the right to vote,
Know you are a feminist.
(I am a feminist)

If you believe a woman have the right to work,
Know you are a feminist.
(I am a feminist)

If you believe that a woman has a right to her
own identity and freedom outside of her
husband or her father,
Know you are a feminist.
(I am a feminist)

If you believe a woman has the right to say no,
without reprisal,
Know you are a feminist.
(I am a feminist)

If you believe that a woman has a right to her
own finances,
Know you are a feminist.
(I am a feminist)

If you believe that a woman has the right to
choose if and when she has a child,
Know you are a feminist.
(I am a feminist)

If you believe that a woman has a right to sexual health,
Know you are a feminist.
(I am a feminist)

If you believe that girls have the same rights to education as boys,
Know you are a feminist.
(I am a feminist)

If you believe that all children should be allowed to grow up to be whatever or whoever they want to be,
Know you are a feminist.
(I am a feminist)

If you believe a man should be allowed to show emotion without criticism,
Know you are a feminist.
(I am a feminist)

If you believe the gentleman in the room are often the strongest men in the room,
Know you are a feminist.
(I am a feminist)

If you believe that all men and all women have a right to make decisions for own their lives,

Know you are a feminist.
(I am a feminist)

If you believe that this is the way it should be all
over the world,
Without exception,
Know you are a feminist.
(I am a feminist)

To graciously acknowledge the change between
your life and your ancestor's lifetime,
is to be a proud feminist.

To be a feminist is to believe in elevating one
another and embracing our differences.
Regardless of gender
Without agenda
For all genders

To be a feminist is to know that education and
kindness takes more strength than violence and
hatred.

Feminism is not a gender
It is equality for a better society
There is no debate
There is no devil's advocate
To believe differently is to surrender to a
propaganda designed by fear

To perpetuate a divide
Designed to keep men and women
Apart, at war and at their worst
To believe differently is to discredit your own
efforts,
Your own history
And deny your alliances

To believe differently keeps us separated, angry
and unsupported.
Feminism is not a gender.
Feminism is not agenda

Safe

I keep myself safe
So, I've created a safe space I call home,
To keep myself safe
That's what women are supposed to do after all.

I keep myself safe,
I don't take risks others might,
So I keep myself safe
From the evils of the night.

I keep myself safe,
I know what I should and shouldn't do
To keep myself safe,
Women can't make mistakes like men do.

I keep myself safe
Safe because I know the dangers that do exist,
I keep myself safe
Because I know the reality of all this.

I keep myself safe.
I plan out how to get there and how to get
home,
Keeping yourself safe isn't as easy as let's just go
with the flow.

I keep myself safe,
Watching the pour of every drink,
To keep myself safe,
From what someone might decide to put in it.

I keep myself safe,
I lock all the doors and check them twice
To keep myself safe
And I still can't sleep at night.

I keep myself safe
Because what else can you do,
When you're only just surviving the
consequences of what not living safely will do.

I keep myself safe
Because in the end no one else can,
So, I keep myself safe
Because there's only me the courts will blame
If I don't keep myself as Safe
As I possibly can.

I keep myself safe,
I watch for alarm bells and warning signs,
Till in the end they obscure any love
Of any kind.

Now I'm so fucking safe,
Surrounded by a sea of red flags,

No one can even see me
Or how unsafe I feel most of the time.

But still, I keep myself safe,
Even though I rage in my mind
With the consequences of what this safety has
developed and entwined.

I keep myself safe
Because it's frightening out there.
So, I keep myself safe
By accepting this life I have here.

I keep myself safe
Safe from what could possibly unfold.
So, to make sure I'm safe,
I make out I'm OK with being alone.

I keep myself safe
In this prison I call home
But at least it keeps me safe Being a woman on
my own.

I keep myself safe
When I'm alone here in the night
Keeping myself Safe
By not taking the Risk
Those out there living might.

It's not good enough

Wandering back from a late night out On the
last train home from Somewhere,
Who knows where?
Does it matter where?
I don't know.

I'm all dressed up,
Boots, skirt, the works... and I wonder,
Am I asking for it?
There are a few people about but it's late, and I
can't help but feel
Suddenly
Vulnerable.

I walk past a group of guys on the platform and
they look at me.
And I wish I had a coat.
But it's warm and I didn't want to carry one.
Was that stupidity?
They think the attention is a compliment.
And I can't quite place why it feels...
So
Predatory.

I 'm sure that they don't mean any harm.

They've just had a few drinks and are heading
home to their wives, girlfriends, women they
love,
Why would they care about me? Right?
Why would they care about me?
Boys will be boys, right?
Especially after a few beers with the lads, right?
Boys will be boys.

Some guys get on the train.
They keep looking my way, making comments
and giggling,
Smacking their lips and shouting out. 'Hey!'
I feel sick.
They say, 'we're just being friendly, joking
around'.
'What's up baby?'
'Why so miserable today?'

Because this is a compliment, right?
There's no need to freeze, right?
No need to hold my breath, like I'm drowning
Lost at sea...
Right?
Fight or flight.
Should I get off this train?

I've got a second to split but I'm frozen and my
mind cannot decipher between present danger
and that ever constant fear women have lived
with since the dawn of time.
And now the doors are closing

And the choice is no longer
Mine...

The train finally reaches my stop.
I'm walking home when some guy appears from
Nowhere
He's cat calling after me as I walk down my
street.
Getting closer and louder
As the street gets longer and darker.
Does he think that this is a compliment?
Does he think that this is.. alright?

It's not good enough to know that no means no,
If you are still waiting for the drunkest girl in the
bar to say yes.
It's not good enough to understand 'Me Too',
Whilst bragging about the girl you got your way
with last night.
It's not good enough that you defend your
daughters, mothers, sisters, girlfriends and
wives,

If you are still not understanding what is and what isn't intimidating to the girl heading home on her own.
It's not good enough to be shocked at horror in the headlines
Whilst manipulating the next bed in which you will lay.

It's not good enough to know that you are not a rapist
If you are still, STILL!!!
Behaving this way!

The Lockdown

Riding The CoronaCoaster

Lockdowns got my head in a spin.
Like a dog who got stuck chasing its tail,
I don't know where I end and where I begin.
Overthinking things that should come so
naturally
Like which direction I should be moving in
And which can only lead to tragedy.
But this whirlwind I got caught in keeps
redirecting me
And I don't know whether to follow my heart Or
listen to my head and think practically.
Should I be productive to my training
And think financially,
Or surrender unto my art
And live minimally...
But passionately.

If I could stop for a second and break out of this
calamity
Then maybe I could access some kind of sanity
But the lack of stimulation
Is deadening.

My lockdown nails metaphors for the state of
things.
I drag their broken edges against my skin just to
feel something.
Coz it's been so long since I touched another
human being
I sometime wonder if the things I'm seeing
Exist in a shared reality
Or if I've slipped into an unconscious state of
being
And this is a nightmare I've made out of my own
nihilistic profanity.

It's like I'm stuck in the middle lane behind a
Prius,
I know I'm going somewhere but the journey's
become slow and tedious.
And the hypocrisy of people standing on their
doorstep clapping for the NHS
Who one year earlier voted in a party ready to
drain it of its public spends,
Is driving me in directions I think would be
better missed.
So, I escape living vicariously through some
Netflix plot twist.
As days merge into days with atrophy,
Slipping through our fingers with uncertainty,
Clamouring just to find something to hold on to
Longing for a life I can feel some connection to.

Coz some days I feel alright
But some days I can hardly remember why I
bother.
Trying to keep perspective and remembering
that there are nations who live permanently
with pandemic horrors.
Losing touch with the person that I used to be,
Striving to make it count and not let it all slip
away from me.
Like a nightmare you can't wake up from.
Remembering that gratitude is the best way out
of this melancholic hum drum.

I guess, I'm just looking for some hope
In a world that feels so hopeless.
Seeking out the starlight to guide me through
the darkness.
A mad scramble of thoughts searching for a
lifeboat,
To stop themselves from drowning in an ocean
full of delusional consorts.
Because this night has been going on too long
now.
Pulling at my survival skills like a drowning man
without the know-how.
Sinking under the weight of it all,
Coz I'm out of my mind exhausted with being
strong now.

I don't even know if I wanna survive this crisis.
If the new normal is to exist inside this
disconnected silence.
Coz I was never frightened of a virus,
I just don't want to have anything to regret
when my time comes.
So, if there's a lesson I'm supposed to learn then
just let me learn it,
So, I can go back to living in a world where I can
try and earn it.
Fighting for the things that I believe in.
And make some kind of contribution as a
worthwhile human being.

I'm not looking for the answers,
Just a place where I belong.
Like I did before the world turned upside down
and my clothes all started fitting wrong.

Trees grow into forest even in the most
challenging of soils
By adapting to their environment and
maintaining connections through their hardest
turmoil's.
And if we are really honest
Aren't we all just characters in this cosmic
master plan?
Nursing some illusion that we are superior to
The knowledge that nature spans.

Existing in her echoes of the love she gave so free.
Clawing at Mother Nature,
Till she found herself empty.

And if perhaps the pandemic
Is her portal to acceptance and peace.
Maybe we could all take a leaf from nature And the evolution her struggles teach.

On Endings

Am I old

Am I old?
Has my body betrayed me?
Nationalised my youth
While I was distracted by its seductive
ephemerality.

Am I that lady at the end of the film
Looking back nostalgically?
Having lost years between memories
and plans?

Like sand through an egg timer,
Has the trickle slowed to those remaining
grains?
Sifting slower now
With more intentionality
More mindfulness
Seeking endlessly for purpose and reason to
make sense of the mysteries that have passed

Have the years accumulated
Leaving me with more behind
Than are placed in front of me now?

We rejuvenate
7 by 7
Till one day we don't recognise our own
reflection.
Laughter lines
And the tell tell signs
of lost evenings spent masquerading the
facades of a youthful sinner

Am I wise?

Is wisdom worth more than the commodity of
youth?
In a world that glorifies naivety and flawless
skin,
Self-destructive behaviours and those who
would cause harm to themselves in an effort to
consistently look like their Instagram.

Would you do it all again?
Knowing what you know now?
Would you take the same risks?
The same lazy mornings?
The same stresses and worries?

Would you maintain the same relationships?

What would you change if you could?

Am I brave?

Did I allow myself the space
To make mistakes
Did I give myself the freedom to be reckless
Without being careless
To be expressive
Without being thoughtless
Was I open to growth

Did I seize opportunities?
Did I laugh off my failures
Just to get up and try again in a different way?

Would I alter any of the decisions that I'd made?

Am I loveable
Have I cultivated an environment to which
others are drawn?
Am I desirable?
Have I expressed interest in the lives of others in
balance to interest they have shown?

Did I love with all the passion in my heart and
Let go with all the grace in my soul

Did I make a difference without expectation
Did I care when I had nothing to personally gain

Am I old?
Have I danced across the hands of time
for the final time?

Would I be afraid if I did?
Or would I take comfort
In the retrospect of living the life that I have
lived?

Farewell Love

In the wake of love stands grief,
The bigger the wake,
The greater the love,
Deceased.

But don't cry for me,
I'm only going home.
It's as it was always meant to be,
I'm only going home.

Leaves fall into the earth
As they turn from green to brown
Decaying back into the muddy ground
From which they first were formed.

As to shall I return to source that gave me my
life and death
So don't cry for me,
I'm only going home.

For what is space both near and far When you
are in fact my heart.
For time as we all know it now
Shall seem like only moments
We were apart.

Epitaph

There'll be no flowers
When I go.
Don't waste your money.
Don't steal them
From their homes,
In which they thrive
And grow.
Don't fritter away their lives
With knowledge,
That your actions will only speed up their own
inevitable tragedy To also wilt and die.

There'll be no sorrow.
No place for regret.
No time for tears.
No what ifs, if only's or what could have been's.
Don't dream of me.
Don't wish me well.
Don't remember my name as a reason for grief.
Don't carry out in sadness as the reasons for
missed opportunities.
Because,
I have nothing to regret!

Because of all things that have come to pass,
I can say that I have truly lived!
For now, I have travelled to a place beyond

And in your joyous memories.
And merry, gleeful songs.
I will find that place of peace in which I can rest.

But capture my words,
For that when I disappear
You will not let this fight die.
And that life may be breathed into the hearts of
those it has been careless with, Long, long after
I have gone.
'Hope springs eternal for those unafraid to try'.
And should my body,
So frail to emotion
And the brutality of this world,
Relinquish control and surrender unto the
earth.
I shall rest in peace,
With the knowledge, That
It wasn't all for nothing.

Final Words...

If you can imagine it, you can achieve it

I climbed up
To a place that's high,
Just to see if I could fly.
To see if I just believed
That if I could grow wings,
That I could really sore the skies.
To see if it
Was just a belief
That told you anything is true.
That if you can imagine it,
You won't believe what you could do.

I climbed on high,
On high,
On high,
For fear the ground might ensue
And chase me up into the skies
With a campaign of its own pursuit.

I climbed up to
Where I could Escape
From what the world had to offer.
If I could climb just high enough

Perhaps I could leave behind this horror.

I climbed and climbed
Till I could touch the clouds, Till I could breathe new air.
I climbed until the night drew in,
Till I almost ceased to care.

And when the sight below looked like
Tiny toys trapped inside a looking glass,
I set a fire to all I had to lose
And let go of what had passed.
I took all my hopes and fears and dreams
And moulded them into one.
And in that highest state that I could reach,
I collided with every one.

And as the ground rose up to meet me,
Expanding clarity with every view.
I overflowed with such serenity
Believing fate would face me soon.

Out of my exhausted mind and with nothing left to lose,
I reached out wide and took to the skies
And now I know it's true.
That if you can imagine it
You won't believe what you can do.

Kilha McQueen is a London born writer and poet who works as a Child and Adolescent psychotherapeutic counsellor specialising in working with teens from challenging backgrounds, helping them make sense of their stories through creative interventions.

Having written since she was very young, she now performs independently on the London spoken word scene as well as being the creative inspiration for the monthly @poetics_open_mic shows held in London.

Poetics aims to offer young poets a safe space to find their voices alongside the supportive expertise of more established poets and provides a vital Therapist in Residence service for their outreach programs bringing therapeutic poetry writing workshops to the spaces where they are needed.

For a selection of her work or to get in contact she can be found on Instagram @kilhapoetry or kilhamcqueen@gmail.com

For outreach work in schools or youth clubs please contact poetics.ltd@gmail.com
Please feel free to get in touch.

Printed in Great Britain
by Amazon

86205461R00132